# beauty magic

101 recipes, spells, and secrets

# beauty magic

by Jennifer Knapp  illustrations by Amy Saidens

**CHRONICLE BOOKS**

SAN FRANCISCO

Library of Congress Cataloging-in-Publication Data:
Knapp, Jennifer.
Beauty magic : 101 recipes, spells, and secrets / by Jennifer Knapp.
p. cm.
Includes index.
ISBN 0-8118-4222-3
1. Beauty, Personal. 2. Beauty culture. 3. Charms.
4. Incantations. 5. Magic. I. Title.
GT499.K53 2004
646.7'26—dc22
2003023606

Manufactured in China

Designed by Amy Gregg

Distributed in Canada by Raincoast Books
9050 Shaughnessy Street
Vancouver, British Columbia V6P 6E5

10 9 8 7 6 5 4 3 2 1

Chronicle Books LLC
85 Second Street
San Francisco, California 94105
www.chroniclebooks.com

## acknowledgments

These products were tested on friends and boyfriends, not on animals. Many thanks to the amazingly creative Mikyla Bruder, Leslie Davisson, Lisa Campbell, Leslie Jonath, Amy Saidens, Vanessa Dina, Steve Kim, Jan Hughes, and Doug Ogan.

# mirror, mirror on the wall
## who's the fairest of them all?

You are, my glamour-puss! And if that's not what your mirror
says when you drag yourself to the bathroom each morning,
don't risk seven years of bad luck by flinging the stupid thing
out the window. Better to enchant that smart-alecky mirror,
and everyone else, with some modernized beauty magic—your
very own bewitching charms and ancient potions—concocted
by you, and possessing all the power of the ages.

*Beauty Magic* helps the aspiring beauty goddess with an
enchanted make-up bag of recipes from the ancient innovators,
traditional healers, and kitchen experimenters, all mixed
up with a modern twist. Each collection of recipes features
a selection of irresistible top-to-toe treatments to suit your
desires.

Treat yourself like a queen with the mysterious allure of Cleopatra's Secrets. Pampering goodies include a pore-refining Nile Mud Mask (page 25) and a Sparkling FireFly Massage Bar (page 28), each scented with a modern version of an ancient perfume. Feeling like a trip to the sun-kissed coast? Flip to Tropical Sun Goddess and open the fridge. You'll probably have everything you need to create a Traditional Lulur Ritual balm (page 44) or a soothing Sandy Foot Scrub (page 50). Add a fluffy beach towel, a pile of mindless magazines, and a kiddie pool and soon you'll feel the ocean breezes blowing. No time for glamour today? Gasp! There is always time with Glamour on the Go. Get moving with a few quick-to-mix treats, including One-Minute Magic Coffee Gloss (page 112) and On-Your-Toes Foot Spritz (page 117). In the mood to dance under the stars? Throw a big handful of glimmer into the mix and get ready with Midsummer Night Treats. Glam it up with Titania's Fairy Dust Eye Glitter (page 121) and Moonstruck Kissing Balm (page 123). After all that brewing, relax with the rejuvenating recipes in Glamour Goddesses. Refresh your body and mind with Venus's Magic Cream (page 144) and Flora's Blue Chamomile Face Serum (page 147).

If magic is to be had, your hand-mixed potions are sure to possess their own unique hocus-pocus. So whip out your magic mascara wand, bombshell, it's time to summon the muses for a spell of *Beauty Magic*.

# the bare-naked basics

Before stirring up a bubbling cauldron of glamorous goodies, take
a few minutes to acquaint yourself with the basics of kitchen
concocting. Stock up your kitchen with a few simple tools and a
selection of ingredients from these lists and informational charts.
A little prep time will make your mixing go smoothly and help you
avoid any emergency trips to the store. Finish up by reading the
tips on technique and safety and you're ready to grab your apron.

## equipment

A few simple kitchen tools will make your mixing a snap. You may want to
consider having a set of kitchen equipment for cosmetic brewing only.
That way, you won't end up with lavender-flavored meatloaf or macaroni
& cheese scented lip gloss.

Ceramic or glass mixing bowl

Various small ceramic or glass bowls (microwave-safe)

A double boiler (enamel is the best choice; metal can react with some
ingredients)

Measuring spoons

Measuring cups for dry and liquid ingredients

Wooden spoons

A fine sieve

A mixer (an immersion hand mixer, sometimes called a stick mixer, is
best, but a regular hand mixer, a blender, or even a whisk works just fine)

A spice grinder or a mortar and pestle (optional)

A funnel

## ingredients

A few core ingredients make up the recipe basics and provide a pantry for
your own experiments. After you're familiar with these ingredients, begin
to try more exotic components. Soon your laboratory will be full of
irresistible potions and charms.

## liquid oils

Oil and water form the basis of most lotions and creams. Liquid oils add texture to the mixture while imparting moisturizing and therapeutic properties to the skin. Full of vitamins and antioxidants, certain oils are believed to encourage healing and cell growth. Choose at least two base oils for your potions.

Almond oil—Emollient, light, good for all skin types
Apricot kernel oil—Light, skin softening, easily absorbed, good for mature and dry skin
Jojoba oil—Nongreasy, easily absorbed, similar to skin sebum, odd scent

## butters

Semisolid at room temperature, creamy butters thicken and enrich your concoctions. They are very emollient and nourishing for the skin, sealing in moisture and forming a barrier between you and those nasty outside elements. Choose one semisolid oil for your creams.

Mango butter—Semisolid, rich, emollient
Coconut oil—Semisolid, moisturizing, makes cosmetics fluffy
Shea butter—Semisolid, nourishing and moisturizing, slightly richer than mango butter and coconut oil

## waters

Along with oil, water is the most important cosmetic basic. It thins oil and other ingredients for lighter, more spreadable potions while hydrating the skin. Mix water with rose petals or fragrance for extra zip. Because of its presence in just about every recipe, choose pure bottled, filtered, or distilled water. Tap water with chlorine and other chemicals can be drying to skin and react with the other ingredients. Aloe vera is soothing and healing to the skin; it can be used to replace water in a recipe for a richer mixture.

Filtered or distilled water—Pure water is the best for cosmetic use
Rose water—Rose-infused water, good for all skin types, and it smells nice too
Aloe vera gel—Emollient gel from the aloe vera plant, very skin soothing

## solidifiers, texturizers, and waxes

These natural ingredients add a truly magical touch, imparting texture and stability to your mixtures. A dash of these key ingredients will produce creamy creams, smooth lotions, and stable balms. If you're looking for products like the ones you buy in a cosmetics store, stock your pantry with these basics.

Beeswax—The best wax around, handmade by our industrious, buzzy friends. Make sure to find pure, cosmetic-grade wax, not a candle-making blend.

Cocoa butter—A brittle wax, adds a hardening texture to mixtures; emollient for skin, and a yummy chocolate scent

Emulsifying wax—Derived from vegetables; binds water and oil

Stearic acid—Derived from vegetable fat; thickens and emulsifies

Liquid vegetable glycerin—A natural humectant and texturizer

*Lotion Tip: This tip applies to all lotions containing emulsifying wax. As with baking, it is best to have all ingredients at a similar temperature when mixing lotion. To keep the waxes from seizing up when you add the water, use hot water in the recipe. If your wax does coagulate, it's no big deal; just realize that you will need to continue to heat and stir the mixture until all ingredients are melted and well blended.*

## essential oils & absolutes

Essential oils are concentrated oils extracted from herbs, flowers, tree barks, resins, and fruit peels. Aromatherapy-grade essential oils are the highest quality. Health food store essential oils are generally good and pure and work well in cosmetics. Absolutes are similar to essential oils but are made with an alcohol extraction process. Fragrance and flavor oils are usually all or partially synthetic and should be used in recipes only as a fun twist. The best-quality ingredients are expensive. It can take pounds and pounds of petals to create a few ounces of oil. If your cranky piggy bank has refused your application for a loan, choose one or two essential oils that you really like and use them in everything. Or use a similar but less expensive scent—for example, opt for orange rather than neroli. Perform a sniff test and choose a few favorites from this list of easy-to-find scents.

| oil | scent | properties |
| --- | --- | --- |
| Bergamot | Floral, citrusy, complex | Uplifting, refreshing |
| Chamomile | Mild, sweet spice | Calming, sedative |
| Cinnamon* | Warm, spicy | Revitalizing, exotic |
| Coriander | Sweet, spicy green | Soothing, clarifying |
| Elemi | Mild, fresh, lemony, complex | Calming, grounding |
| Frankincense | Rich, sweet, balsam | Inspiring, calming |
| Ginger* | Hot, spicy, earthy | Warming, aphrodisiac |
| Grapefruit* | Sweet, tangy, citrus | Stimulating, uplifting |
| Jasmine absolute | Intense floral, sweet, honeylike | Sensual, joyful, relaxing |
| Lavender | Floral, spicy, herbal | Cleansing, relaxing, antiseptic |
| Lemon* | Fresh, clean, citrus | Refreshing, stimulating, astringent |
| Lime* | Bittersweet, citrus, fresh | Refreshing, astringent |
| Myrrh | Fresh, fruity, camphor-like | Calming, meditative |
| Neroli | Warm, floral, sweet citrus | Euphoric, rejuvenating, aphrodisiac |
| Patchouli | Earthy, musky, sweet | Relaxing, sensual |
| Peppermint* | Fresh, cool, zippy | Cooling, refreshing |
| Rose absolute | Floral, deep, warm | Uplifting, regenerative |
| Sandalwood** | Mild, woodsy, sweet | Relaxing, aphrodisiac |
| Tangerine | Sweet, warm, spicy, citrus | Calming, refreshing |
| Vanilla absolute | Smooth, rich, sensual | Harmonizing, aphrodisiac |
| Vetiver | Earthy, smoky, exotic | Grounding, calming |

* skin irritant
** threatened species

Consult an aromatherapy or herbal reference guide for complete
information on these oils and absolutes, and do not use them
while pregnant or nursing.

## herbs, flowers & spices

Herbs, flowers, and spices impart scent and soothing properties to your potions. To boost a beauty potion's glamourizing abilities, always choose the highest-quality ingredients. Medicinal and culinary herbs and flowers are now readily available at health food and specialty stores. Look for colorful, pungent-smelling spices and organic dried herbs and flowers. Consider growing and picking some of your own herbs and flowers for the best results. The aromatic selections in the following list are safe for most people to use externally in cosmetic products. Consult an herbal reference guide for complete information, and do not use these while pregnant or nursing.

| herb | traditional use |
|------|-----------------|
| Calendula | Wound healing |
| Cardamom | Stimulant, aromatic |
| Chamomile | Calming, soothing |
| Cinnamon | Muscle soothing |
| Clary sage | Sedative, aphrodisiac, fragrance |
| Comfrey | Wound healing |
| Elder flower | Anti-inflammatory |
| Eyebright | Eye soother |
| Ginger | Antiseptic, stimulant |
| Lavender | Antibacterial, anti-inflammatory, sedative |
| Lemon balm | Antibacterial |
| Lemon verbena | Sedative, fragrance |
| Mullein | Emollient, astringent |
| Nettle | Astringent |
| Peppermint | Cooling, antibacterial, stimulant |
| Rosemary | Antiseptic, energizing |
| Rose petals | Emollient, regenerative |
| Violet | Anti-inflammatory, eye soothing |

## specialty ingredients

Explore the world of beauty with these unique ingredients that hail from all over the globe. Natural preservatives will help your potions last longer and let them remain unrefrigerated. Or try a specialty essential oil to enrich your potion. These oils have been used traditionally for their amazing therapeutic properties, and are completely optional.

| ingredient | traditional use |
| --- | --- |
| Vitamin E oil | Mild preservative, antioxidant effect, nourishing for skin |
| Grapefruit seed extract | Natural preservative, see package labeling for usage information |
| German chamomile essential oil | Deep blue oil, anti-inflammatory, soothing |
| Everlast essential oil | Skin regenerative, soothing |
| Evening primrose oil | Skin regenerative, smoothing |
| Rose hip seed oil | High in fatty acids, excellent for mature, dry, and chapped skin |
| Mica | Adds sparkle to cosmetics |
| Kaolin clay | Used for facial masks and "mud baths" |
| Chlorophyll | Health supplement |
| China brush | Artist's brush |

# easy infusions

You probably make infusions daily. But perhaps you don't realize it! Tea is the most common water infusion. Infusions are used to impart the scent and therapeutic properties of herbs, flowers, fruit peels, and other natural material to water and oil. Infused waters and oils can be used alone or as an ingredient in cosmetic recipes.

## infused oils

Infused oils can be used alone as subtly perfumed massage or fragrance oils or as part of a recipe. In a pinch they can replace an essential oil; however, they are not as potent. Experiment with your infusions by using a variety of herbs and flowers.

### warm oil infusion

To infuse oils with plant essences, place a few cups of roughly crushed dried herbs and flowers in the top of a double boiler. Cover the plants with a few cups of oil. Heat the oil to 150 degrees and let simmer for at least 1 hour—a few hours is even better. The longer you heat the mixture, the stronger the oil infusion will be. Strain the plant material from the oil and repeat with fresh plant material until the desired strength is achieved.

### cold oil infusion

Place a few cups of roughly crushed dried plant material in the bottom of a large jar and cover with a few cups of oil. Cap the jar and let it infuse for 3 or 4 days. Strain the plant material from the oil and repeat with fresh plant material until the desired strength is achieved.

## infused waters

Infused waters are available in specialty bath shops, with lavender, rose, and orange blossom being the most common. They are also easy to make at home using your favorite flowers. The infused waters can be used in recipes, as toners, or as linen and room sprays.

### cold water floral infusion

If you are using fresh petals, place them between paper towels to wilt overnight. Place one cup of roughly crushed wilted or dried petals or herbs in a jar. Cover with 2 cups filtered water, cap, and let infuse for 3 or 4 days. Pour the water through a sieve, removing the petals and retaining the infused liquid. Repeat with new petals in the same infused liquid until the desired strength is achieved.

### hot water floral infusion

In a saucepan over medium heat, combine one cup of fresh or dried, roughly crushed flower petals or herbs and 2 cups filtered water. Bring the mixture to a boil, remove from the heat, cover, and let steep for 15 minutes. Just like making tea! Pour the water through a sieve, removing the plant material and retaining the infused liquid. Repeat with new petals in the same infused liquid until the desired strength is achieved.

## safety first!

**Patch Test**   Don't jinx yourself before you've started! Even though your lotions and potions will be conjured up using all natural ingredients, your skin may still be irritated by one of your concoctions. Sensitive skin, young skin, old skin, allergy-prone skin, and even perfectly normal skin can react badly to a product or ingredient. Before doing the top-to-toe treatment, test all recipes with a patch test. Dab a small amount of the finished mixture on the inside of your arm and wait for 24 to 48 hours. If any redness, itching, rash, or other unpleasant symptoms occur, forget it! Toss your potion (or give it to a less sensitive friend) and move on to the next.

**Skin Sensitivity**   Many of the essential oils, preserving oils, and other components of the recipes should not be used on the skin unless diluted (in a recipe, for example). Although packed with beneficial qualities, citrus- and spice-based essential oils in their pure state are skin irritants and should be well diluted and used in moderation. Make sure to follow any warnings and directions on the packaging for individual ingredients. With very sensitive skin, it is often best to leave potions unscented.

**Cosmetic Grade**  Always, always make sure you are buying cosmetic- or food-grade products. You don't want to end up scouring yourself with industrial cleanser!

**Time's Up!**  These recipes are fresh and are best used and enjoyed in a timely fashion, so make only what you can use in about 1 month. Although the natural preservatives offer mild protection from spoilage, always keep your creations in a cool spot or in the refrigerator. Most mixtures should remain fresh for at least 1 month. Recipes without preservatives will keep for 1 to 3 weeks in the refrigerator. See the individual recipes for storage suggestions. If any of your ingredients or completed mixtures begin to smell off or strange in any way, it is best to toss them out and start afresh.

**Warning**  Pregnant women, nursing women, people on medication, and young children should not be messing around with herbs and essential oils if they are not an herbologist, a doctor, or a big expert on the subject. Herbs are medicinal, and even some of the most common ones can be dangerous.

# all dolled up

Half the fun of concocting cosmetics is in the packaging. Begin to accumulate plastic bottles, decorative jars, tubs for creams, spritz bottles, and lip balm pots. Many containers are available in specialty stores, health food stores, and on-line. Products that will be used in the bathroom should be placed in plastic containers, gift items should be decked out in gorgeous glass jars, and essential oils and infusions should be stored in dark-colored glass jars and bottles (they can react with plastic and light). Don't forget to decorate your potion containers with customized labels and stickers.

Bottles and jars can be reused but should be sterilized and completely dry before a new fantastic concoction is poured in. You don't want uninvited bacteria spoiling a fabulous potion.

I

# cleopatra's secrets

Modern and ancient scholars alike disagree as to whether
or not the Queen of the Nile was physically attractive. She
certainly was obsessed with the latest potions and with
having perfectly lined cat eyes. Whether she would meet
today's rigid idea of glamour is a mystery. But there is no
question that she possessed the type of overall beauty,
inside and out, that had many high-powered lovers falling
at her feet. Called the Queen of Allure, she was a witty
conversationalist, a well-educated woman who spoke nine
languages, a hostess known for her debauched parties,
and, oh yeah, the leader of a country. Gorgeous!

Treat your body like a temple with a few of Cleopatra's
Secrets, recipes that echo the ancient Egyptian's skills
with fragrance. Simple renditions of the age-old scents
add a mystical allure to each mixture.

Hand mirror
Picture of Cleopatra (or another beauty)
Green candle
Lily fragrance oil

# eternal moon beauty spell

Summon the mysterious radiance of Cleopatra or another beauty you
admire. Draw on her essence with a simple spell and the scent of lily.
Common in beauty products of the time, lilies were the flowers most
associated with beauty in the ancient world. Before setting off on a
trip down the Nile, Cleopatra scented the sails of her boat with lily oil.
Heavenly! Why aren't more women running countries when they
obviously do things so right?

On the night of a full moon, place or prop the mirror on the floor in
such a way that it reflects the moonlight. Place the picture near the
mirror. Drop 3 drops of lily oil on the candle and light it. Repeat the
following incantation 3 times:

> earth, air, fire, sea;
> cleopatra shine through me.

Repeat the ritual for 3 nights in a row. On the third night burn the
picture and visualize the traits you admire transferred to yourself.

1 tablespoon kaolin clay (available at health-food stores)
1 tablespoon honey
1 tablespoon puréed papaya
2-inch-wide china brush (optional)

# nile mud mask

A simple and fresh mask will bring the glow of the desert sun to your
cheeks while nourishing your skin. The healthful qualities of honey
are so profound that the ancients believed it was a gift from the gods,
the tears of Ra. Honey is a natural emollient and humectant, and it
also has antibacterial properties. Papaya contains antioxidants such
as vitamins A and C and is an excellent moisturizer and toner in one.
The natural clay firms the skin and refines pores while drawing out
any impurities. For dry or sensitive skin, omit the clay for a powerful
moisture boost.

In a small bowl, stir together the clay, honey, and papaya until it
forms a paste. Using a china brush or your fingertips, gently spread
a thin layer of the gooey yumminess over your face, avoiding the
eye area. Relax for 15 minutes. Rinse off with warm water, pat dry,
and moisturize as usual. Toss any leftovers.

½ cup boiling filtered water

For normal and dry skin, use 1 tablespoon each dried calendula, chamomile, comfrey, lavender, lemon balm, mullein, and rose petals

For oily skin, use 1 tablespoon each dried parsley, rose petals, rosemary, calendula, and lavender

2 tablespoons aloe vera gel

2 tablespoons liquid vegetable glycerin

2 tablespoons honey

10 drops vitamin E oil (a natural preservative)

Immersion hand mixer (whisk, hand mixer, or blender)

8-ounce bottle

# aloe & honey facial cleanser

The Egyptians were crazy about cleanliness and bathed daily. This was probably necessary, as soap wouldn't be invented for hundreds of years! This gentle and light facial cleanser is infused with a big bouquet of gorgeous flowers, each packing its own magical symbolism and medicinal properties. The soothing and moisturizing benefits are adjusted to suit various skin types.

In a small bowl, pour the boiling water over the flower and herb mixture, cover, and let steep for 15 minutes. Pour the mixture through a sieve into a liquid measuring cup, removing the plant material and retaining the infused liquid. Set aside and let cool. In a mixing bowl, stir together the aloe vera gel, glycerin, honey, and vitamin E oil. Pour a slow stream of infused liquid into the aloe vera mixture while blending with the immersion mixer. When the mixture is smooth and thoroughly blended, decant the cleanser into the bottle and cap.

Store in the refrigerator. The cleanser should remain fresh for 2 or 3 weeks. Shake before each use. Use a small amount of cleanser with water twice a day.

1 cup Epsom salts

1 cup sea salt

1 cup Dead Sea salt

Orange, yellow, and red food coloring

3 tablespoons citric acid

A few drops each cassia, lemon grass, juniper, and myrrh essential oils

24-ounce decorative jar

1 or 2 tablespoons each dried rose and calendula petals

Seashell scoop

# dead sea layered bath salts

Many ancient Greek writings refer with reverence to an important Egyptian tome full of perfume recipes and ingredient information. The original book has never been found, but the author was none other than Cleopatra herself. These soothing bath salts are scented with oils reminiscent of those ancient perfumes. The colored salts are then layered to resemble the arid Sahara sands, with a dash of fizziness thrown in just for fun. Salts gently cleanse and soften the skin and soothe away muscle aches and pains.

In a mixing bowl, stir together the three salts. Divide the salt mixture among 3 small bowls, 1 cup in each. Add a few drops of orange food coloring to one bowl, yellow to the second, and red to the third. Make the salts as pale or as saturated with color as you wish. Using a clean spoon for each bowl, thoroughly mix the color into the salts, and then stir a tablespoon of citric acid into each bowl. Add 1 or 2 drops of each essential oil to all 3 bowls and stir. Pour one bowl of salt into the bottom of the jar and sprinkle in a thin layer of rose petals. Pour in another bowl of salt to cover the petals and add a layer of calendula petals. Top the jar off with the remaining salt, place a seashell scoop on top, and cap.

Add 2 or 3 scoops (or tablespoons) to your bath. Umm!

*Variation: For a blue Nile variation, use blue and purple food coloring and dried lavender.*

1 tablespoon coconut oil

1 1/2 cups cocoa butter

A few drops each cinnamon and sandalwood essential oil and jasmine absolute

1 teaspoon cosmetic-grade mica in a color of your choice

Oval soap molds

# sparkling firefly massage bar

This adorable oval bar twinkles like a firefly, and soon so will you! Tiny flecks of sparkling mica will spread over your skin as the heat of your body melts the bar. It works just like massage oil but without the mess. A ritual unto itself, a single ancient perfume oil took up to 2 years to prepare. The come-hither scent of this bar is a less time-consuming rendition of one of Egypt's famous perfumes—perfect if you're on the fly.

Place the coconut oil and cocoa butter in a microwave-safe bowl and microwave on high until melted, about 30 seconds. Do not overheat. Stir the essential oils, jasmine absolute, and mica into the melted mixture. Pour the mixture into the soap molds and let cool. Unmold and enjoy. Use as an after-sun body balm, or indulge a lucky recipient with a glowing massage. Store the bars in a cool spot.

beauty on the inside:
# healing refreshers

Hippocrates was the first health guru! The ancient Greek philosopher was one of the first to promote the idea that beauty was a product of the body, mind, and spirit. He advocated a nutritious diet and exercise as part of a successful health and beauty regime.

Drinking plenty of water is an important component of any daily routine. A fresh glow, bright eyes, and clear skin are just a few of the benefits to being well hydrated. Whether you're out on your camel in the desert or just sitting in traffic, be sure to drink plenty of water. Too boring for your queenly tastes? Try these flavor-packed refreshers. Fill a large pitcher with filtered water and slice in a whole lemon or tangerine for fresh taste and vitamin C. Grate in some fresh gingerroot or throw in a handful of fresh organic mint. Experiment with your favorite fresh fruits, herbs, and veggies. Always have your refrigerator stocked and a bottle on hand, and you'll get through those 8 glasses a day, no problem.

4 cups boiling filtered water

½ cup each dried lavender, clary sage, and tangerine peel

A few drops each lavender, clary sage, and tangerine essential oils

Natural cotton sheeting cut into 4-inch-wide strips, or cotton bandaging (hand towels will work too)

# egyptian herbal spa wrap

The ancient world was as obsessed with beauty as the modern one is, with many of the beauty and spa treatments we know today invented as long as 6,000 years ago. Scented baths, herbal steams, and perfumed oil massages were common therapies of the time.

This purifying and soothing herbal wrap provides a spa-style steam right in your own bathroom. The herbal blend is known for its relaxing aroma and would have been used in beauty treatments and rituals in ancient times. The steam opens pores, draws out impurities, and leaves you with a healthy glow. Now all you need is a pyramid!

In a mixing bowl, pour the boiling water over the dried lavender, clary sage, and tangerine peel. Cover and let steep for 15 minutes. Pour the mixture through a sieve into another bowl, removing the plant material and retaining the infused liquid. Stir the essential oils into the liquid to strengthen the scent. Add the strips of sheeting to the bowl, cover, and let steep for 5 minutes.

When the water is cool enough to handle, wring out the strips of sheeting one at a time. Wrap your legs and then your body and arms just like a mummy. The sheeting should be snug (but should not cut off circulation!), with each wrap slightly overlapping. Cover yourself with a big, fluffy towel and relax in a warm room for 10 to 15 minutes. Unwrap, pat dry, and moisturize as usual.

2

# kama sutra magic

Many of the most highly prized ingredients in ancient
beauty products were native to India and other Asian
countries. Beauty potions are included among the earliest
known documents. Many of the hot, hot spices, cool, cool
cucumbers, and refreshing yogurts are still used today in
India and incorporated into the principles of Ayurveda.

Ayurveda is one of the oldest wellness philosophies still
in practice. It is a spiritual and medicinal tradition of
well-being begun in India 5,000 years ago. Through diet,
exercise, meditation, and medicinal herbs, a balance of
the mind, body, and outside elements can be achieved.
Beauty is a by-product of general good health or properly
balanced doshas or energy points. Ayurvedic healers
create personalized remedies that take into consideration
a person's unique being as well as the commonality of all
nature. The following recipes are simplified versions,
containing herbs and spices found in the Ayurvedic
tradition that promote general good health.

# beauty temple incense oil

Lure Lakshmi, the Hindu goddess of beauty and good fortune, to your lair with this irresistible scent. While performing your daily beauty ritual or mixing up an exotic potion, burn this beauty-drawing incense in an essential oil burner. The tantalizing aroma will attract beauty to you as well as radiating your mesmerizing masala outward. Carry the scent with you by soaking a strand of sandalwood beads in the oil, polishing them with a soft cloth, and wearing them around your neck.

In a jar, combine equal measures of roughly crushed rose petals, ground cinnamon, ground cardamom, and lemon peel. Pour almond oil over the mixture, cap, and let infuse for 3 to 4 days. Strain the oil through a coffee filter and repeat with fresh plant material if necessary to strengthen the scent. Decant the oil into a dark glass container and store in a cool place.

24-ounce decorative jar

1 cup sea salt (see Note, page 58)

1½ cups almond oil

A few drops each ginger and tangerine essential oils

1 tablespoon finely grated fresh ginger

1 tablespoon cosmetic-grade gold mica (optional)

# fresh ginger scrub

Ginger has been an important ingredient in beauty magic and love potions for thousands of years. Mildly antiseptic, it is believed to possess strong healing powers. This energizing body scrub will leave your body polished, moisturized, and with a provocative spicy scent. A scoop of gold mica adds extra sparkle to the already gorgeous golden scrub. Be warned! All your friends will want a jar for their bathroom shelf.

In the jar, stir together the sea salt, almond oil, essential oils, ginger, and mica. Use a dollop of the scrub in the shower after cleansing. Scrub with a washcloth or your hand, using a circular motion; rinse thoroughly, pat dry, and moisturize as usual. Store the scrub in a cool spot.

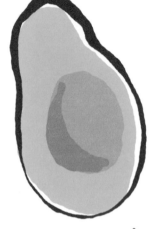

Half an avocado
Half a banana
1 tablespoon bee pollen
1 tablespoon honey
1 tablespoon plain yogurt
2-inch-wide china brush (optional)

# avocado moisture mask

India is known for its arid climate, searing sunny days, and sweltering nights. When your face needs an instant monsoon season, try this extra-rich, vitamin-packed mask. It provides speedy relief and is especially good for normal to dry skin. Avocados are one of nature's miracle inventions; they are a concentrated package of fatty acids and are full of antioxidants. Banana boosts the moisturizing ability of this concoction further, helping plump up fine lines and wrinkles.

In a small bowl, mash together the avocado and banana, using a fork. Stir the bee pollen, honey, and yogurt into the mash. Using a china brush or your fingertips, spread an even layer of the mixture over your face, avoiding the eye area. Leave on for 15 minutes. Rinse off with warm water, pat dry, and moisturize as usual. Toss any leftovers.

# ayurvedic massage oil

A quick way to add a little more joy to your day, a customized bottle of massage oil will tantalize your nose with your favorite fragrance. Aromatherapy is not a new fad; in fact, it's a very old one! Scent cures have been used in India for at least 3,000 years and for up to 6,000 years elsewhere in the world. These therapeutic oils have since been studied by the lab-coat-wearing crowd and proven to tickle all the most sensitive spots of the brain.

Your body and mind will let you know whether you need to relax with bergamot or cardamom, get moving with grapefruit or basil, or get happy with neroli or tangerine. Add a few drops of your chosen essential oil (try a few together) to a half-full bottle of almond oil, cap, and shake. Top it up with almond oil, and shake again.

For an Ayurvedic combination that's as relaxing as a lounge chair, add a few drops each of sandalwood and vetiver essential oils to a bottle of apricot kernel oil.

8-ounce jar

6 tablespoons apricot kernel oil

2 tablespoons dried rose petals

2 tablespoons broken cinnamon sticks

4 crushed cardamom pods

2 tablespoons jojoba oil

1 tablespoon emulsifying wax (derived from vegetables)

1 tablespoon stearic acid (derived from vegetable fats)

$1\frac{1}{2}$ cups warm filtered water

Immersion hand mixer (whisk, hand mixer, or blender)

A few drops each cinnamon and tangerine essential oils and vanilla absolute

$\frac{1}{4}$ teaspoon vitamin E oil (a natural preservative)

Two 8-ounce bottles

Labels and stickers (optional)

# cinnamon & vanilla body lotion

The dash of spicy cinnamon in this creamy lotion warms and scents the skin while relieving any muscle aches and pains. The combination of cinnamon and vanilla has been used since ancient times to encourage love and amorous antics. It has since been proven that this fragrance stimulates the feisty portion of the brain. Omit the spices if you have more than enough honeys already or if you have sensitive skin, for a nice, basic, everyday body lotion.

In the jar, pour the apricot kernel oil over the rose petals, cinnamon, and cardamom. Cover the jar and let infuse for 3 to 4 days, or if you're a want-it-now sort of person, make a warm oil infusion (page 18) instead. Pour the oil mixture through a sieve into a small bowl, removing the plant material and retaining the infused oil.

In a double boiler set over simmering water, stir together the infused oil, jojoba oil, emulsifying wax, and stearic acid until melted. Pour a slow stream of the water into the oil mixture while stirring. When the mixture is smooth and thoroughly blended, remove it from the heat. Using the immersion hand mixer, blend in the essential oils, absolute, and vitamin E oil until the mixture is fluffy and thickened. Decant the lotion into the bottles, let cool slightly before capping, and label if you wish. Stored in a cool spot, the lotion should stay fresh for 1 month. Shake before each use if necessary.

Note: Cinnamon essential oil has many benefits, but like all essential oils, it is very strong and concentrated in its pure form and has the potential to irritate some people's skin. When mixing up this recipe for the first time, begin by using a small amount of cinnamon essential oil, perform a patch test (page 19), and then carefully add a bit more oil if you wish.

beauty on the inside:

# belly-dancing bauble

In times past, from Mayan palaces to Greek temples, the ability to create a beautiful work of art was more admired than a pretty face. Release your creative energy by making a jeweled anklet, using the colors and stones long associated with beauty spells and rituals. Green is the color most connected with beauty across cultures; look for small crystal beads in your favorite tone. Find a few beads of jade, malachite, olivine, opal, and red jasper. These stones are closely connected with beauty magic. String a simple strand of your chosen treasures on a stretchy filament fiber (available in bead shops). Slip it around your ankle and show it off with a few belly wiggles.

# 3

# tropical sun goddess

If you live in the northern climes, it is inevitable that at some point in the long, gloomy winter the cute woolly cap and stripy scarf that looked so cozy last autumn are, after months of dedicated service, just irritating and itchy. Suddenly, you feel the overwhelming urge to free yourself from the layers of entangled, scratchy sweaters and emerge goddesslike in a string bikini with an umbrella-festooned drink in one hand and a trashy novel in the other.

If your piggy bank doesn't share your romantic notion of a holiday in Tahiti, rediscover traditional island rituals with a few of these magically sun-kissed recipes. One whiff of these beachy scrubs and splashy spritzes will whisk you off to a tropical beach, even on a rainy day.

The unique and age-old beauty traditions of the islands—unusual spices, fresh tropical fruits, and exotic nut oils—are only as far away as your local health food store.

1 cup jojoba oil

2 tablespoons rice flour

2 teaspoons ground turmeric

1 teaspoon sandalwood powder

A few drops ylang-ylang essential oil, frangipani fragrance oil, or jasmine absolute

$1/4$ cup almond oil scented with your favorite tropical essential or fragrance oil

2 cups plain yogurt

$1/2$ cup fresh frangipani or jasmine blossoms

# traditional lulur ritual

The *lulur*, an Indonesian beauty ritual, is performed on a bride each day of the week leading up to her wedding. If you don't have a week, just a single treatment will leave you refreshed and ready to take on a new life (or your new, improved old one) with sweetly scented skin.

In a small bowl, stir together the jojoba oil, rice flour, turmeric, sandalwood powder, and essential oil until the mixture forms a paste (add a few drops of water if necessary to thin). Massage your body with the almond oil, rubbing toward the heart. Then smear the turmeric paste over your body, from neck to toe. Let dry. Rinse in a warm shower, rubbing the dried paste off using your hand or a loofah in a circular motion to exfoliate, and pat dry.

Rub the cooling yogurt over your body. Relax for 15 minutes, and then rinse in warm water. Run a bath and add the flower petals for your final cleanse. Hop in, twirl your toes in the air, and imagine being fanned with palm fronds.

Be aware that the turmeric, especially after repeated treatments, can leave a yellowish tint on the skin. This tone is gorgeous on olive skin but possibly not so great on winter white. Don't worry, no one will notice when you're all bundled up.

Half a mango, puréed
Half a papaya, puréed
¼ cup coconut yogurt
1 tablespoon honey
2-inch-wide china brush (optional)

# island fruit enzyme mask

When your skin is as blah as the weather, treat it to this tropical pick-me-up. Fruit enzymes are antioxidants that neutralize all the bad free radicals in your skin, leaving it exactly as it should be, balanced and revived. Papaya is a moisturizer and toner in one delicious package. Full of vitamins, it refines pores and helps heal blemishes. Mango is full to the brim with vitamins A, E, and potassium to moisturize. Yogurt is an emollient and contains gentle milk acids to encourage exfoliation.

In a small bowl, stir together the mango, papaya, yogurt, and honey until well blended. Using a china brush or your fingertips, spread the mixture over your face, avoiding the eye area. Leave on for 15 minutes. Rinse off with warm water, pat dry, and moisturize as usual. Discard any of the leftovers or gobble them up; this particular recipe is just as good for your insides!

1/2 cup mango butter

2 tablespoons jojoba oil

A few drops of your favorite essential or fragrance oil; try something tropical, like ylang-ylang, gardenia, lime, tangerine, jasmine, banana, or coconut

8-ounce jar

# mango body butter

This buttery body balm is perfect for a day at the beach or as a treat for parched skin after too much sun. Mango butter is a rich emollient oil from the plant's seeds. Jojoba is derived from a tropical bean and is actually a wax that closely resembles the body's own sebum. That may sound sort of icky, but it is actually very good because it doesn't clog your pores. Scent your butter with a tropical oil such as irresistible ylang-ylang. Known as an aphrodisiac, it is used to scent South Sea bridal beds.

In a double boiler set over simmering water, stir together the mango butter and jojoba oil until melted. Remove from the heat and stir in the essential oil until smooth and thoroughly blended. Pour the butter into the jar and let cool slightly before capping. Store in a cool spot.

*Variation: This recipe is a perfect opportunity to experiment with tropical nut oils. Replace the jojoba oil with kukui nut or macadamia nut oil. These nut oils are high in fatty acids and are sunburn soothing and skin regenerative.*

1 pomegranate

1 cup aloe vera gel

3 tablespoons cornstarch

2 tablespoons witch hazel

$\frac{1}{2}$ cup jojoba wax beads or strawberry seeds
(see Note, page 58)

5 drops grapefruit essential oil

3 drops lime essential oil

3 drops tangerine essential oil

1 drop lavender essential oil

Two 8-ounce decorative jars

# pomegranate gel scrub

Pomegranate is the fruit of the goddess Venus and has long been associated
with love, lust, and beauty, thanks partly to its naughty, red juiciness. Its
beauty benefits are more tangible: pomegranate juice has been found to
have the highest level of antioxidants of any juice. And we all know why
antioxidants are our friends. This particular scrub is perfect for all skin
types, but problem skin will especially appreciate the oil-free exfoliation.

Separate the juicy seeds of the pomegranate from the peel and place the
seeds in a sieve. Using the back of a spoon, squeeze the juice through the
sieve into a bowl. Measure 2 tablespoons of the juice into the top of a double
boiler set over simmering heat and add the aloe vera gel, cornstarch, and
witch hazel. Stir until thickened and an opaque red. Remove from the heat
and let cool. Pour the mixture through a sieve into a bowl, removing any
solids and retaining the gel. Stir the jojoba beads and essential oils into the
aloe vera mixture. Spoon the scrub into the jars. Use a dollop daily, to exfoliate
in the shower. Store in the refrigerator and stir before using. The mixture
should remain fresh for 2 to 3 weeks.

Half a banana
1 tablespoon honey
1 teaspoon avocado oil

# banana hair pack

This delicious, moisturizing hair treat will leave your hair so full of joy the only danger is that it might just bounce right off your head doing its happy dance. Pack this on your hair before shampooing for deep, penetrating moisture that will condition your scalp and leave your hair shiny, soft, and without a tangle in sight.

In a small bowl, mash the banana, honey, and oil together with a fork. Before shampooing, apply the mixture to your hair, distributing it from the scalp to the ends. Wrap your head in a towel and relax for 20 minutes. In the shower, rinse out the mixture, shampoo, and condition your hair as usual. Toss any leftovers.

¼ cup beach sand
¼ cup almond oil
10 drops vitamin E oil
10 drops tea tree oil
A few drops each peppermint, spearmint, and rosemary essential oils
4-ounce jar

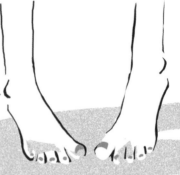

# sandy foot scrub

Feet are probably one of the most underappreciated parts of your body. They provide years of devoted schlepping, and for what? To be ignored, bundled up in smelly socks, and forgotten. Well, it's high time to give them a treat, to spruce them up and let them strut their stuff.

Sneak home a few handfuls of fine white sand from your next beach holiday. When mixed with cooling peppermint and invigorating spearmint oils, the sandy scrub will rejuvenate your feet and make them feel as though life is worth living. The tea tree oil will banish any unwelcome guests that have taken up residence between your twinkle toes.

In a small bowl, stir together the sand, almond oil, vitamin E oil, tea tree oil, and essential oils. Pour the mixture into the jar. Gently rub a dollop of the mixture over your feet, using a circular motion and really scrubbing any callused or knotty areas. Rinse your feet in cool water, pat dry, and rub on tons of moisturizer.

Note: Sea salt or sugar can be substituted for the sand in this recipe.

1 tablespoon watermelon juice
2 tablespoons aloe vera gel
Two 1-ounce containers

# watermelon sun soother

Watermelon and aloe combine in this super sunburn soother. Smooth this gel over red areas to cool and nourish the skin while providing protection for healing.

In a small bowl, stir the watermelon juice into the aloe vera gel. Pour the mixture into the containers. Stored in the refrigerator, the gel should last for 1 month.

beauty on the inside:
# summoning laka, goddess of the hula

Fun begets happiness, and a huge smile is always beautiful. Have some fun and add to your talents by learning a hula dance or two. Each dance tells a story, so find one that means something in your life. Bring a ray of sunshine into your world anytime and anywhere by taking a class or renting a how-to video. Wiggle those hips!

# pagan princess

Throughout pagan times and the middle centuries, the freshly scrubbed look was the height of fashion, or nonfashion. Poverty and growing religious intolerance dictated that cosmetic "paints" were for prostitutes (and, okay, also for rich people in France). But medieval maidens weren't giving up quite so easily. They mixed up their own potions right in the kitchen from favorite recipes they collected and traded. Practitioners of pagan magic concocted remedies and then passed their knowledge of herbal lore and healing down through the ages. Herbal mixtures known for their beautifying properties combined with humble ingredients, such as milk, oatmeal, brown sugar, roses, and other common kitchen staples, to form delightful, sweet-smelling skin care basics.

Discover your inner Pagan Princess with ingredients straight from your kitchen pantry. These fresh-from-the-mixing-bowl recipes will nurture your skin and boost your natural radiance.

# celtic spring
## beauty ritual

Beltaine, or May 1st , is one of the two most important celebrations on the Celtic calendar. Like many pagan festivals, it is basically all about merrymaking. Summer is welcomed with bonfires, dancing, feasting, and stolen kisses! Many smaller rituals are performed on the day as well, including this one: On Beltaine morning, preferably before dawn, a maiden should wash her face in the morning dew. This will create radiant, youthful beauty throughout the year while ensuring health and happiness.

The very best dew is to be found on the hawthorn tree. Each tree has important symbolic meaning in Celtic lore; the hawthorn is associated with the White Goddess, Andraste, and promises hope, pleasure, and protection. Water from this day—dewdrops, raindrops, and flowing spring water—should be saved in vials and used throughout the year to add a Celtic kick to your mix.

¼ cup grated castile or glycerin soap base
¼ cup lemon juice
2 tablespoons almond oil
2 tablespoons cream of tartar
1 or 2 tablespoons rosemary blossoms
or very finely chopped leaves
6-ounce ceramic ramekin or box

# lemon & rosemary soap

This typical kitchen recipe for soft, creamy citrus soap made its first cookbook appearance in the 1800s. It is undoubtedly a much older traditional recipe that remakes leftover soap into a charming soft cleanser. Lemons have been associated with love charms and beauty rituals since the earliest of times. Native to India, they spread to the Middle East and Europe thousands of years ago through trade. Lemons refresh and even the skin tone, and rosemary is toning and good for all skin types.

In a double boiler set over simmering water, stir the soap until melted. In a small bowl, stir together the melted soap, lemon juice, almond oil, cream of tartar, and rosemary until it is the consistency of honey. Pour the mixture into the ceramic ramekin or box. Scoop out a small amount to use as a refreshing hand or body cleanser.

1 cup powdered milk
1 cup dried rose petals
A few drops rose essential oil

# milk & roses bath

This bath was meant to nurture the milk-and-roses complexion
every Celtic maiden desired. The fragrant mixture is actually
healthful for all complexions, dark or fair. Milk naturally softens the
skin but also contains gentle acids that encourage skin regeneration.
Roses have been an integral part of beauty spells and love charms
since the earliest times. They are the flowers of Venus, the goddess
of love and beauty, and are appropriately beautifying with both
emollient and rejuvenating qualities.

In a small bowl, stir together the powdered milk, petals, and
essential oil. Pour the entire mixture into a warm bath, slip in, and
hum a Highland jig.

12-ounce decorative glass jar
1 cup brown sugar
1/2 cup almond oil
8 drops vanilla absolute (or your favorite essential oil)

# blissful **brown sugar** scrub

With this recipe you'll look sparkling clean and radiant, and you'll smell just slightly of freshly baked cookies. Be prepared to be gobbled up!

Loosely fill the jar with the sugar. Pour the almond oil over the sugar and stir in the absolute. Scoop out a handful of scrub during your shower, and rub it over your body, using a circular motion, to exfoliate. Delicious!

Note: Try making your own exfoliants for your scrubs. Oatmeal, rice, dried beans, nuts, rinsed and dried fruit seeds, and cornmeal make great skin-polishing grains. Experiment by running one or two through a clean spice grinder until you find the right grit.

1 cup old-fashioned oatmeal
1 tablespoon dried lavender
Washcloth or cheesecloth
1-foot length of green ribbon

# gentle oatmeal facial milk

If you have sensitive, red, chapped, broken-out, or generally grumpy and unhappy skin, try this soothing oat milk compress. Oat milk gently cleanses while moisturizing. Replace your usual cleanser with this treatment for a few days to encourage your skin to naturally improve its mood. Lavender is excellent for the skin and uplifting for the senses. Tie the compress with a green ribbon to attract beauty and rebirth.

In a small bowl, stir together the oatmeal and lavender, and pour the mixture into the center of the cloth. Gather the corners together and tie tightly with the green ribbon. Soak the sachet in a sink full of hot water for 5 minutes. Squeeze the bundle several times between your fingers to release the oat milk. Dab the bundle over your face, or use it as a compress on irritated areas. Rinse your face with the oat-infused water from the sink, pat dry with a soft towel, and moisturize if necessary.

1 tablespoon apricot kernel oil

1 tablespoon jojoba oil

1 tablespoon emulsifying wax (derived from vegetables)

1 tablespoon stearic acid (derived from vegetable fat)

1 tablespoon liquid vegetable glycerin

1 cup filtered water

2 tablespoons aloe vera gel

1/2 cup rose water, purchased or homemade (see Floral Infusions, page 19)

Immersion hand mixer (whisk, hand mixer, or blender)

10 drops bergamot essential oil

5 drops geranium essential oil

1/4 teaspoon vitamin E oil (a natural preservative)

12-ounce bottle

# three flowers moisturizer

This lotion is light to the touch but rich in the good stuff. The flower oils are fantastic for the skin and they smell nice too; rose is emollient and restoring, bergamot encourages a rosy glow, and geranium minimizes pores.

In a double boiler set over simmering water, stir together the apricot kernel oil, jojoba oil, emulsifying wax, stearic acid, and glycerin until melted. In a small bowl, stir together the water, aloe vera gel, and rose water. Pour a slow stream of the water mixture into the oil mixture while stirring. When the mixture is smooth and thoroughly blended, remove from the heat. Using the immersion hand mixer, blend in the essential oils and vitamin E oil until the mixture is fluffy and thickened. Decant the lotion into the bottle, let cool slightly before capping, and label if you wish. Stored in the refrigerator, the lotion should remain fresh for 2 to 3 weeks. Shake before each use, if necessary.

beauty on the inside:
# dreamtime pillow

Although late nights are fun on occasion, a few winks are what suits your health. A long and deep sleep will leave your mind sharp and your body fortified and looking its best. A pungent mix of flowers and a dash of spice will send you directly to the land of nod with its sleep-inducing scent. Fill a small sachet pouch with a few tablespoons each of dried hops, whole cloves, broken cinnamon sticks, lavender, lemon balm, and chamomile. Tie the bag with a green ribbon for beauty, and tuck it into your pillow.

Note: If a new baby is interfering with your sleep, fill a sachet with dill, lavender, and chamomile. Secure it safely inside the tiny tyke's crib bumper, and you'll both get to know the sandman better.

# mermaid magic

Although they may exist only in the realm of magic and myth, mermaids have been known to inspire a few down-to-earth (or out-to-sea!) potions for natural beauty. Waterproof mascara gets you only so far, whether you're a water baby or a landlocked siren. Refreshing deep blue marine blends make the most of the ocean's mineral-rich plants and soothing salts. These treasures should not just be left to the fishes.

The mysterious image of the mermaid, comb and mirror in hand, inspires the following luxurious beautifiers, many for your lovely locks. Deep sea flora and a pinch of sea salt enhance your shiny mane, whether you have a fish tail or not.

# message-in-a-bottle spell

Create a message-in-a-bottle beauty spell to send out to
sea or set on your Boudoir Altar (page 82). Find a small,
decorative bottle, and fill it two-thirds full with corn syrup.
Now sprinkle in the beauty magic. Using an indelible-ink
pen, write a thought or phrase that makes you feel beautiful
on a small slip of paper. On another slip write down
something you'd like to work on internally or externally.
Place the two messages back to back and stick a piece of
tape over the front and back. The tape should completely
cover the messages so they are watertight. Tie a piece of
love-inducing red ribbon around the messages. The beauty
you possess will help you attain the beauty you desire.

Place the messages in the bottle, sprinkle in a pinch of
glitter, some plastic jewels, a piece of beauty-drawing jade,
and a drop of Beauty Temple Incense Oil (page 34), all the
while concentrating on the messages. Top up the bottle
with water, cap, and shake vigorously until well blended.
Anytime you would like to invoke the spell, shake up the
bottle and let the magic swirl.

2 tablespoons seaweed powder
1 tablespoon aloe vera gel
1 to 2 tablespoons cooled mint tea
2-inch-wide china brush (optional)

# seaweed & mint tea facial

If you've been lounging around in the hot sun harassing sailors all day, refresh your skin with this cooling mask. Mineral-rich seaweed combines with soothing aloe and refreshing mint tea for a skin-softening potion that will feel like a plunge into the deep sea.

In a small bowl, stir together the seaweed powder and aloe vera gel. Slowly add just enough mint tea to thin the mask to a spreading consistency. Using a china brush or your fingertips, gently spread a thin layer of the mixture over your face, avoiding the eye area. Relax for 15 minutes. Rinse off with cool water, pat dry, and moisturize as usual. Toss any leftovers.

1 cup boiling water

2 tablespoons each dried rosemary, yarrow, nettles, horsetail, and comfrey

2 tablespoons powdered seaweed

¼ cup liquid castile soap

1 teaspoon fractionated (liquid) coconut oil or almond oil

1 teaspoon vitamin E oil (a natural preservative)

5 drops each lemon and grapefruit essential oils and carnation absolute

12-ounce bottle

# luscious locks shampoo

When all that's covering your ta-tas are your lovely locks, you want them to be extra luxurious. Rosemary is beneficial for all hair and scalp types and will say bon voyage to any small microbes or sea monkeys lurking around. Yarrow is stimulating, nettles and seaweed are vitamin and mineral rich, horsetail is astringent, and comfrey is emollient and healing.

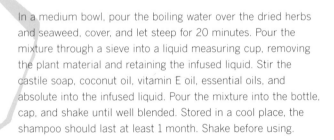

In a medium bowl, pour the boiling water over the dried herbs and seaweed, cover, and let steep for 20 minutes. Pour the mixture through a sieve into a liquid measuring cup, removing the plant material and retaining the infused liquid. Stir the castile soap, coconut oil, vitamin E oil, essential oils, and absolute into the infused liquid. Pour the mixture into the bottle, cap, and shake until well blended. Stored in a cool place, the shampoo should last at least 1 month. Shake before using.

¼ cup jojoba oil

1 tablespoon coconut oil

1 tablespoon emulsifying wax (derived from vegetables)

1 tablespoon stearic acid (derived from vegetable fat)

2 cups filtered water

Immersion hand mixer (hand mixer, blender, or whisk)

10 drops lime essential oil

5 drops lavender essential oil

¼ teaspoon vitamin E oil (a natural preservative)

12-ounce bottle

# deep sea hair conditioner

We all love a fluttery sea breeze, but sometimes it can leave your hair
looking more like you had an encounter with an electric eel. Calm
your hair down with a wave of moisture and an airy scent that will
transport you directly to the shores of the Mediterranean.

In a double boiler set over simmering water, stir together the jojoba
oil, coconut oil, emulsifying wax, and stearic acid until melted. Pour
a slow stream of the water into the oil mixture while stirring. When
smooth and thoroughly blended, remove from the heat. Using the
immersion mixer, mix in the essential oils and vitamin E oil until
thickened. Decant the mixture into the bottle and let cool slightly
before capping. Shampoo hair, apply conditioner, wait a few
minutes, and rinse well. Stored in a cool spot, the conditioner
should remain fresh for 1 month. Shake before using, if necessary.

1 cup liquid castile soap
8-ounce bottle
A few drops blue food coloring
2 teaspoons blue or green cosmetic-grade mica
A few drops cucumber or gardenia fragrance oil

# ocean sparkle body wash

If you're a stylish mermaid and soap is just too humdrum, mix up a bottle of this gorgeous ocean bath gel. Castile soap is the gentlest of cleansers, and when mixed with a fresh scent there is no better way for your skin to start the day.

Pour the liquid castile soap into the bottle until half full, add the food coloring, mica, and fragrance oil, and cap and shake well. Top up the bottle with the remaining soap, cap, and shake again until well blended.

*Variation: Add a few tablespoons of sea salt to your body wash for a gentle exfoliating rub.*

3 cups mixture of 3 types of dried seaweed (wakame, hijiki, ogo, whichever you like)

1/3 cup rice vinegar

1/2 cup light sesame oil

1 tablespoon sugar

1 teaspoon chili paste

1 teaspoon grated fresh ginger

1/4 cup sesame seeds

A drizzle of tamari or soy sauce (optional, depending on the saltiness of the seaweed)

## beauty on the inside:
# super seaweed salad

Seaweed is concentrated goodness for the body. After slathering it all over your outside, it's time to load up inside. It's a diet staple among many coastal cultures, and for good reason: it is packed full of fiber, enzymes, amino and nucleic acids, minerals, trace minerals, and almost every vitamin in the alphabet. Eaten daily, the benefits of glossy hair, luminous skin, and overall good health should become apparent in a few months. This yummy and crunchy salad is a delicious toe-in-the-water introduction to seaweed cuisine.

In a mixing bowl, pour water over the seaweed until completely covered. Let the seaweed soak until rehydrated, 20 to 30 minutes. Drain and rinse the seaweed. Using a kitchen towel, pat it dry. Cut the seaweed into thin strips, removing any stems, and set aside.

In a salad bowl, whisk together the vinegar, sesame oil, sugar, chili paste, and ginger until the sugar dissolves. Add the seaweed and toss. Sprinkle with the sesame seeds and drizzle with tamari or soy sauce to taste. Yummy!

# uzume beauty

Uzume is the Japanese goddess of merriment. She is known for her happy hijinks—dancing naked is one of her favorites, something everyone should try at least once. A happy inside is the best beauty secret and the most natural. Call on Uzume to put a huge smile on your face while throwing together a few of these giggly charms.

Uzume Beauty mixtures take advantage of the beautifying benefits of traditional Asian herbs, flowers, and teas.

# amaterasu spell

Amaterasu is the Shinto sun goddess. She spends most of her days hot-rodding around the skies on her racy red dragon. She enters the earthly realm through mirrors, looking at her beauty and that of others before returning to her heavenly hang. Draw on her powers with this beauty manifestation charm. The spell brings all your inner beauty to the surface. Your good qualities will become part of your outer appearance and apparent to your many admirers.

On the night of the waxing moon, sit facing a mirror in a darkened room. Sprinkle ginseng and orange blossoms in a circle in front of the mirror. Place a lighted red candle in the circle and concentrate on the qualities of your inner self you'd like to release. Extinguish the candle without blowing. Then brush your hair until the air is flashing with static electricity. Repeat this incantation.

**amaterasu come to me;**
**inner beauty, be set free.**

Half a cucumber

½ cup rice flour

2 tablespoons adzuki bean meal

2 tablespoons honey

2 tablespoons aloe vera gel, or more if necessary

1 tablespoon seaweed powder

A few drops vetiver essential oil

2 sheets nori

2 tablespoons fresh or dried elder flowers

Bento box (optional)

Plastic grass garnish (optional)

A few tablespoons water or liquid vegetable glycerin

# sushi roll facial

These facial rolls look just like sushi—those little packets of fishy heaven. In fact, these rolls are so cute that you might find yourself too busy admiring your handiwork to use them as intended. In such cases, serious action must be taken. Wrap up a bento box of facials for a deserving pal so that someone benefits from the emollient rice, exfoliating adzuki bean meal, refreshing cucumbers, calming vetiver, and mildly astringent elder flowers.

Using a paring knife, peel the cucumber and cut it in half lengthwise. Remove the seeds, cut the cucumber into long, thin strips, and set aside. In a small bowl, stir together the rice flour, adzuki bean meal, honey, aloe vera gel, seaweed powder, and essential oil until it forms a paste, adding more aloe vera if necessary to thin. Very lightly toast a sheet of nori and spread half of the rice flour mixture along one end of the nori. Place a few cucumber strips and half of the elder flowers along the center of the rice paste. Roll up the nori with the rice paste, cucumbers, and elder flowers inside, just like a sushi roll. Dab the end of the nori with water to seal, and cut into 1-inch slices. Repeat with the other sheet of nori. Place the pieces on their ends in a cute bento box with a plastic grass garnish, if you wish. Just like sushi, your facial will need to be refrigerated. They should remain fresh for 1 week.

To use the facial, unroll one or two rolls and remove the cucumber. Thin the rice paste mixture to spreading consistency with 1 to 3 tablespoons of water or glycerin. Spread the mixture with the elder flowers in an even layer over your face, avoiding the eye area. Place a strip of cucumber over each eye. Relax for 15 minutes. Remove the cucumbers and rub the rice paste off, using a circular motion to exfoliate. Rinse with warm water, pat dry, and moisturize as usual.

beauty on the inside:
# beauty treats

Herbal teas are full of healthful properties and an easy addition to your daily routine. A few of the teas known to promote beautiful skin are burdock, stevia, yellow dock, green tea (to rejuvenate), bergamot (to cleanse), black alder (to soothe), and dandelion (to calm breakouts). Replace coffee with a cup of tea for a healthier complexion in a few weeks.

In Japan, adzuki beans are used in many beauty treatments, especially in facials as exfoliants. They also beautify from the inside, reducing puffiness, alleviating under-eye circles, and brightening the complexion. You may not have noticed that these unassuming and unusual beans have become a health food store staple, available both dried and canned. Make your favorite bean soup recipe and replace the usual beans with adzuki beans. Eat an adzuki bean dish once a week to enjoy their beautifying benefits.

1 cup boiling water
1 tea bag green tea
1/4 cup peach nectar
1 packet (1/4 ounce) unflavored gelatin
2-inch-wide china brush (optional)

# green tea & peach peel-off mask

There is something very satisfying about ripping off a fruity mask and starting afresh. With antioxidant-rich green tea and moisturizing peach, this mask deep-cleanses your pores and removes any dead skin cells. Beware! Peach is linked with love magic, so you'll have extra vavoom.

Pour the boiling water into a cup containing the tea bag and let steep for 10 minutes. Remove the tea bag and measure out 1/4 cup of tea. In a double boiler set over simmering water, stir together the tea, peach nectar, and gelatin until the gelatin dissolves and begins to thicken, 1 to 2 minutes. Refrigerate the mixture for 30 minutes. Using a china brush or your fingertips, spread a thin layer over your face, avoiding the eye area. Let the mask dry. Peel off the mask, rinse with cool water, pat dry, and moisturize as usual. Toss any leftovers.

Note: Vegetarians, vegans, and other health-conscious animal lovers should look for vegetable-based gelatin made from agar agar at Asian markets and health food stores.

Lipstick in your favorite color

1 teaspoon beeswax

1½ teaspoons coconut oil

1 tablespoon jojoba oil

A pinch of cosmetic-grade mica in a color of your choice

Three ¼-ounce lip balm pots or two ½-ounce balm containers

# pink pearl cheek gloss

A whisper of sheer glimmer across your cheeks is all you need to brighten your blush while still looking au naturel. Adjust the amount of lipstick to achieve a color that works for you.

Using a paring knife, slice off a thin sliver of lipstick, about ⅛ inch thick. Place the lipstick, beeswax, and coconut oil in a microwave-safe bowl, and microwave on high until melted, about 1 minute. Do not overheat. Stir the jojoba oil and mica into the melted mixture. Pour the mixture into the lip balm pots and let cool completely before capping.

Swipe a stripe of sparkle across your cheekbone or dab a ruby circle on the apple of your cheek.

Note: For a luxurious twist with authentic Japanese flair, replace the mica with crushed pearl powder, available at some Asian markets.

Lipstick in your favorite color

1 teaspoon beeswax

1½ teaspoons coconut oil

1 tablespoon almond oil

A few drops cherry flavoring oil (or your favorite essential oil)

A pinch of cosmetic-grade mica in a color of your choice

Three ¼-ounce lip balm pots

# cherry blossom gloss pot

Laughing behind her fan, a demure *onna–noko* of ages past enhanced her smile with fruit stains. This gloss reinvents that subtle cherry sheen. Free your lip balm from its boring existence as a chapped lip soother, and glam it up with a bit of wink-wink and a little cherry bomb flavor. It will be just as healing but way more smoochable.

Using a paring knife, slice off a thin sliver of lipstick, about ⅛ inch thick. Place the lipstick, beeswax, and coconut oil in a microwave-safe bowl, and microwave on high until melted, about 1 minute. Do not overheat. Stir the almond oil, cherry flavoring, and mica into the melted mixture. Pour the mixture into lip balm pots and let cool completely before capping.

Note: Everybody has a different idea of the ideal lip balm consistency. If the last two recipes are too glossy, add more beeswax for a firmer, stay-put balm.

1½ cups brewed green tea
¼ cup borax
1 cup grated castile soap
A few drops peppermint essential oil
Ceramic container or ramekin

# green tea & peppermint gel soap

Vitamin-rich green tea and stimulating peppermint will invigorate your skin while gently cleansing and brightening your complexion. The soap's soft jelly gooeyness feels great on all body parts, so spread the goodness around!

In a saucepan, bring the green tea to a boil. Add the borax and castile soap, stirring until the ingredients are melted and thoroughly combined. Remove from the heat and add the essential oil. Pour the mixture into the container. Stored in a cool spot, the soap should last for 1 month.

Note: Some people are allergic to borax. In such cases, aloe vera gel may be used as a replacement. Add the aloe vera gel after removing the pan from the heat. Store the soap in the refrigerator for a cool treat.

# 7

# parisian potions

When you conjure up an image of Paris in your mind, what do you see? The Eiffel Tower, scrumptious pastries, women in pretty shoes sitting in cafés, frilly undies, and perfumeries? Whatever the particulars, the overriding image is one of romance, style, and beauty, *ma chère*. Known for their famous perfumes, Parisians have an elegant touch and an appreciation for the very best ingredients that make even the simplest potions more of a romantic dream than a tangible product. *Très jolie!*

The purest scents and sweetest flowers make up Parisian Potions with divine powders, tantalizing perfumes, and kissable potions.

# boudoir altar

As every bewitching beauty knows, an altar is indispensable for mixing up magic and mayhem. If you don't already have a fancy French dressing table, sweep the crazed clutter off any small table and place it against a wall. Set a mirror on the table, or hang one on the wall behind it. Burn a chip of copal on an incense coal to cleanse the table of any ugly scenes in its past life. Cover the top with a green cloth for beauty and rebirth. Now you will need to add items to the table that represent the four elements and ensure balance in your spells. A small bowl or bottle of floral water represents, well, water; a Sweet Dreams Beauty Candle (page 120) embodies fire; a bowl of Linden & Vanilla Dusting Powder (page 85) symbolizes earth; and Beauty Temple Incense Oil (page 34) conveys air. Apply your potions at this table for extra hex appeal.

1 cup baking soda

½ cup citric acid

½ cup cornstarch

2½ tablespoons almond oil

2½ teaspoons water

½ teaspoon mixture of orange essential oil, gardenia fragrance oil, and rose absolute

¼ teaspoon borax (optional; may irritate sensitive skin)

A few drops of red food coloring

¼ cup dried rose petals

Soap molds

Baking sheet

# fizzy champagne bath blasters

Pop the bubbly with a heavenly scented bath buzz. These fizzy treats are almost as much fun to make and give away as they are to use. Emollient salts soothe the skin, while the floral bouquet sends you on a quick trip to the Luxembourg Gardens during a spring rain.

In a large mixing bowl, stir together the baking soda, citric acid, and cornstarch and set aside. In a small bowl, stir together the almond oil, water, essential oils, and borax until the borax dissolves. Slowly add the wet ingredients to the dry, being careful not to let the mixture fizz up. Stir in the food coloring and flower petals. Firmly pack the mixture into soap molds. Carefully unmold the tablets onto a baking sheet. Let the tablets dry slowly for 1 or 2 days. Use one or two per bath, and store the remainder in a watertight container.

Note: To make professional-looking spherical bombs, look for clear plastic snap-together Christmas tree ornaments at the craft store. Pack both sides of the ornament with bath blaster powder, squeeze the two sides together, and then carefully twist to unmold.

$1/2$ teaspoon beeswax

2 tablespoons almond oil

12 drops or more lemon verbena essential oil

Two $1/2$-ounce balm containers

# lemon verbena solid perfume

Stinky cheese and perfumeries! Simple products transcend the ordinary by making the most of the highest-quality ingredients. Use the best essential oil available for this balmy day in a jar. Keep a few tins of this sunshiny fragrance on hand—in your handbag, in the car, and at your desk—for anytime you need a stroll down the long avenues of the Tuileries.

Place the beeswax in a microwave-safe bowl, and microwave on high until melted, about 1 minute. Do not overheat. Stir the almond oil and essential oil into the melted beeswax. Add more essential oil if you wish. Pour the mixture into the balm containers. Let cool completely before capping. Dab a bit behind your ears, on your wrists, everywhere.

Note: Any scent will work well in this recipe. The oil base assures that the fragrance will last without fading. These little pots make great gifts!

½ cup arrowroot powder

¼ cup French white clay

2 tablespoons baking soda

A few drops each linden fragrance oil and vanilla absolute

½ teaspoon cosmetic-grade glitter or mica

8-ounce powder shaker

# linden & vanilla dusting powder

As beguiling as a lingering glance and just as powerful, this fancy boudoir dusting powder will keep you fresh all day. The innocent romantic scent of linden and vanilla is balanced with a pinch of scandalous shimmer. Ooh la la!

In a small bowl, stir together the arrowroot, clay, baking soda, essential oil, absolute, and glitter. Pour the mixture into the powder shaker or into a bowl with a big pink powder puff, *bien sûr*.

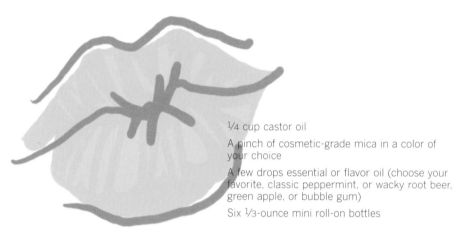

¼ cup castor oil

A pinch of cosmetic-grade mica in a color of your choice

A few drops essential or flavor oil (choose your favorite, classic peppermint, or wacky root beer, green apple, or bubble gum)

Six ⅓-ounce mini roll-on bottles

# french kiss roll-on gloss

Super shine for sloppy kisses. Your pout will beg to be whisked off for a weekend on the Rive Gauche, where it can be smooched in the style it deserves.

In a small bowl, stir together the castor oil, mica, and flavor oil. Decant the mixture into the roll-on bottles, pop in the roller ball, and cap. It's really that easy. Wah-lah!

1 teaspoon coconut oil

1/2 cup cocoa butter

2 tablespoons ground almonds

2 tablespoons medium-coarse sea salt

A few drops each ginger, patchouli, and sandalwood essential oils

Soap mold

# bottom buff

The bottom! There it is, following you around like a lost puppy. But instead of turning around and cooing "oooh sooo cute!" you ignore it, pretend it doesn't exist, or even wish it would go away. That's enough to give any body part an inferiority complex. Maybe if you gave it a little love, after all the comfy seating it's provided you, you might just be surprised at what a little attention accomplishes. This exfoliating massage bar is designed especially for the bottom; it moisturizes, exfoliates, and gets the blood flowing, which is necessary for smoothing away any blobby bits.

In a double boiler set over simmering water, stir together the coconut oil and cocoa butter until melted. Remove from the heat and stir the ground almonds, sea salt, and essential oils into the melted mixture. Pour the mixture into the soap mold. Let cool and unmold. Massage the bar over your thighs, bottom, and hips, using a circular motion. Then jog around the block just for good measure!

3/4 cup boiling water

1 tablespoon each dried lavender, violet flowers, and violet leaves

2 tablespoons jojoba oil

1½ teaspoons emulsifying wax (derived from vegetables)

1½ teaspoons stearic acid (derived from vegetable fat)

1½ teaspoons liquid vegetable glycerin

Immersion hand mixer (whisk, hand mixer, or blender)

10 drops German chamomile essential oil

10 drops evening primrose essential oil

5 drops lavender essential oil

¼ teaspoon vitamin E oil (a natural preservative)

Two 4-ounce containers

# violet eye cream

Lacking that certain joie de vivre? Maybe it's just your tired peeps. Brighten your outlook on life with this light but highly effective cream. The flower oils de-puff and smooth out any fine lines around the eyes. Brilliant blue German chamomile is an anti-inflammatory, and evening primrose is a skin regenerative. Look out! These oils are expensive, but the results are gorgeous, no?

In a small bowl, pour the boiling water over the lavender, violet flowers, and violet leaves; cover, and let steep for 20 minutes. Pour the mixture through a sieve into a liquid measuring cup, removing the plant material and retaining the infused water. Set aside.

In a double boiler set over simmering water, stir together the jojoba oil, emulsifying wax, stearic acid, and glycerin until melted. Pour a slow stream of the infused water into the oil mixture while stirring. When the mixture is smooth and thoroughly blended, remove it from the heat. Using the immersion hand mixer, blend in the essential oils and vitamin E oil until the mixture is fluffy and thickened. Decant the lotion into the containers and let cool slightly before capping. Stored in a cool spot, the cream should remain fresh for 1 month. Shake before each use, if necessary.

beauty on the inside:
# romantic reads

Fill your mind with beautiful images. First, find a suitably romantic flower-specked grassy field, and spread a picnic blanket. Then indulge in the luscious prose of a classic French novel. Look for works by Colette or George Sand—romantic, gorgeous, weepy, and full of that famous je ne sais quoi. Gobble a few bon-bons, guzzle Champagne, let your imagination wander, and pour more Champagne.

# flower power

The sixties had the right idea with the whole peace, love, and flowers groove. Flowers contain tons of good plant vibes that make your body and spirit happy. Spread their flowery love and powerful punch all over your body. Get back to nature, girl.

Pluck a big bouquet of your favorite blossoms to mix up a rainbow of colorful potions with the recipes in Flower Power. Softly scented petals are full of skin-soothing qualities and fresh fragrance.

6-inch square of flower-print fabric

A pinch each dried anise, cowslip, dill, flax, lemon peel, and magnolia

A chip of mirror

A chip of amber

A drop of milk

3 drops jasmine essential oil

6-inch length of green ribbon

# gypsy magic pouch

Filled with the herbs, flowers, and stones linked to beauty in gypsy lore, this little talisman will draw beauty of the body and mind toward you while radiating your lovely presence outward. Carry the charm with you as a reminder to love your body and treat it right.

On a Friday, the day of Venus and the most effective day to cast love and beauty spells, place the fabric square on your Boudoir Altar (page 82) and light the Sweet Dreams Beauty Candle (page 120) and the Beauty Temple Incense Oil (page 34).

Clear your mind of the things-that-need-doing list and concentrate on the elements of beauty you would like to draw and would wish others to see in you. Slowly place each ingredient onto the center of the fabric square. Trap the spell by gathering up the corners of the fabric and tying it with the ribbon. Keep the pouch close to you at all times.

¼ cup liquid vegetable glycerin

1 or 2 drops alcohol-based flavor extract (optional)

1 or 2 drops food coloring

A pinch of cosmetic-grade mica in a color of your choice

Twelve ⅓-ounce glass mini roll-on bottles

A few drops essential or flavoring oil (try blueberry, melon, or cotton candy)

¼ cup castor oil

# groovy roll-on lip gloss

This super-psychedelic lip gloss looks just like a lava lamp. It's even more fun, though, because it *is* lip gloss rather than a boring, old, sit-around-on-a-table lamp. When you tip the tube and roll it on, the action begins, as amoebic blobs of colored goo drift around the tube in a slow-motion cosmic dance. Put on the Hendrix and enjoy the show, all while moisturizing your lips. Right on!

In a small bowl, stir together the glycerin, flavor extract, food coloring, and mica. Pour the mixture into the roll-on bottles until each is half-full, and set aside. In another bowl, stir together the essential oil and castor oil. Top up each bottle with the scented castor oil. Add the roller ball and cap. Turn the bottle upside down and witness the groovy effects. Ooh wow, man.

2 cups filtered water

For normal skin, 1 tablespoon each dried rose petals, lavender, and lemon balm

For dry skin, 1 tablespoon each dried comfrey, chamomile, calendula, and rose petals

For oily skin, 1 tablespoon each dried peppermint, lavender, and rosemary

Bath towel

# summer of love facial steam

Open the pores and free the spirit. Well, at least free the skin of all the impurities that bombard your face each day. The flower-and herb-infused water is balanced for each skin type and will leave your skin clean, fresh, and bursting with moisture.

In a saucepan, bring the water to a boil, add the herbs, reduce the heat, and simmer for 5 minutes. Pour the mixture into a large, heat-resistant bowl, and hold your hand 12 inches above the bowl to test the heat. When the steam is warm but not searing, place your face 12 inches above the bowl, and drape your head with a towel to form a mini-steam room. Relax for 10 to 15 minutes, rinse with cool water, pat dry, and moisturize as usual.

3/4 cup filtered water

2 tablespoons rose water, purchased or homemade (page 13)

2 tablespoons witch hazel

A few drops of your favorite fragrance or essential oil (try rose absolute, jasmine absolute, freesia, or honeysuckle)

8-ounce spritz bottle

# free love flower spritz

When you need a refreshing splash, but the swimming pool forgot to come to the party, mix up a bottle of this cheery floral spritz. Keep a small bottle on hand for a skinny-dip anytime.

Pour the water, rose water, witch hazel, and essential oil into the spritz bottle, cap, and shake well. Spray a mist over your body after your morning shower, or on your face (eyes closed!) for a quick refresher throughout the day. Stored in the fridge for an extra-cool splash, the spritz should remain fresh for 1 month.

beauty on the inside:
# spread the love

When you're feeling inspired inside and out, spread the glam glow around. Volunteer an hour a week at your favorite charity, fill a soup bowl at the shelter, walk a dog at the Humane Society, drive a little old lady to the store (with the red lipstick and powder, they are full of fab beauty tips!). No time this week? Make a donation instead, clean out the closet, unload the cans from the back of the cupboard, or knit a scarf. You'll get back more than you give—guaranteed.

beauty on the inside:
# nature girl

Time to exfoliate your green thumb and get back to nature, all in the name of beauty, of course. Loofahs, those spongelike, scrubby, mystery things, don't come from the ocean, as many suppose. They are actually gourds that can be grown right in your own backyard. The seeds can be purchased at garden centers, some health food stores, and through mail-order seed catalogs. Loofahs grow well in areas that have at least 4 months of warm weather, although they can be given a head start indoors. Similar to squash, they need a sunny spot in which to spread or an arbor on which to climb.

2 cups (16 ounces) coarsely chopped
glycerin soap base

A few drops of your favorite essential oil
(match the scent to the flower, or try
something citrusy)

Soap molds

Almond oil

Plastic, fabric, or natural dried and
pressed flowers

# flower power soap

Hey, you hippie! These soaps will keep hands and bodies oh-so-clean
and smelling like a great big Dr. Seuss flower. Hunt down some
cartoony plastic flowers to float in the middle of each happy soap.

Place the soap in a microwave-safe bowl and microwave on high,
stirring at 1-minute intervals, until melted. Do not overheat. Stir the
essential oil into the melted soap. Lightly rub a small amount of
almond oil into each of the soap molds. Pour in the melted soap,
filling each mold only half-full. Let cool for 5 to 10 minutes. Place a
flower in each mold and top up with the remaining soap base. Let
cool. Unmold and store in a jar, or wrap individually in plastic wrap.

# coven slumber party

Gather the girly-gang and focus your bewitched energy into creating a few delicious goodies. These decadent dessert-like potions may look good enough to eat, but please control your sweet tooth. They are really meant to indulge your body in a different way by nourishing your skin.

Mix a cocktail, dish it with the dames, and enjoy mixing up and sharing a few yummy, pastry-shop-inspired treats full of chocolate, strawberries, and candy-scented oils.

# divine party trick

Let me see what is to be. Kick off the party with a quick divination reading. Buy a pack of tarot cards, pull out the instructions, and get in some practice. Sort out the major arcana cards; this gives you only 22 cards to worry about. Memorize the cards' meanings or write a cheat sheet on your palm. When the guests arrive, give each friend a quick reading.

Have the person cut the deck using her left hand. Your victim should all the while concentrate on a question or problem. She can blurt it out (after a few cocktails) or remain coy. Pull the first 3 cards off the deck and place them in a row. Flip the first card face up. This card relates to what has been going on in the past; it indicates recent influences on the situation. Flip up the second card; it represents the crux of the situation or question. The third card reveals the future, the outcome, what might have an influence soon, and things to consider.

Explain each card as you go along, and then come up with a mysterious, mystical summation of all the elements. If you can't remember all the cards' symbolic meanings, use your intuition to weave an amazing story culminating in a trip to Marrakech or the winning of a pony, and everyone will be happy.

1 tablespoon chocolate chips (use your favorite, semisweet or milk chocolate)

½ tablespoon cocoa butter

1 tablespoon beeswax

½ cup almond oil

Twenty ¼-ounce lip balm pots

20 small stickers (optional)

# chocolate chip lip treat

This moisture-rich balm will protect and soothe your lips—that is, if you can keep from licking it off right away. It makes enough for the chocolate-loving coven plus plenty to keep for yourself. Yum!

In a double boiler over simmering heat, stir together the chocolate chips, cocoa butter, beeswax, and almond oil until melted. Pour the mixture into the lip balm pots and let cool completely before capping. Add stickers to the caps, if you wish.

## beauty on the inside:
# chocolate-dipped fortune cookies

Who can resist breaking into a fortune cookie to discover their fate? "You will win a trip to Paris, where you will stumble upon a fabulous and cheap apartment, write a critically acclaimed but controversial novel, and start a band." Right. Well, if you're really clever you can use tweezers to extract the boring fortunes from store-bought cookies and insert your own really good ones. Chocolate makes everything better, so why not combine the two?

In a double boiler set over simmering water, melt 1 to 2 cups (8 to 16 ounces) of chopped chocolate or chocolate chips. Remove from the heat. Using your fingers, dip a premade fortune cookie into the chocolate, with the opening facing up. Immediately turn the cookie upside down and let the excess chocolate drip back into the pot. The goal is to coat the outside of the cookie while not allowing too much chocolate inside. Place the cookies on a rack to cool.

½ cup strawberries
2 tablespoons yogurt
1 tablespoon cornstarch
½ teaspoon honey
1 or 2 drops lavender essential oil
2-inch-wide china brush (optional)

# strawberries & cream mask

Strawberries contain salicylic acid, a scary name for a helpful fruit acid that gently sloughs off dead skin cells, relieves itching, and zaps blemishes before they can even think about crashing this party. Despite the powerful ingredients, the mask is cooling, soothing, and feels great. Strawberries are meant to be shared, so buy a few extra pints for nibbling; they are known to bind romantic love and friendships. Apply this mask to all the partygoers for a real spa experience, and don't forget to take the necessary goofy photos.

In a small bowl, mash the strawberries with a fork. Stir the yogurt, cornstarch, and honey into the strawberry mash. Add the lavender oil to the mixture and blend well. Using a china brush or your fingertips, spread the mixture in an even layer over your face, avoiding the eye area. Relax for 15 minutes. Rinse with warm water, pat dry, and moisturize as usual. Toss any leftovers.

24-ounce bottle natural, unscented baby shampoo

Three 8-ounce bottles

A few drops red food coloring

A pinch of cosmetic-grade mica in a color of your choice

A few drops each almond essential oil and vanilla absolute

Labels and stickers (optional)

# bon-bon bubble bath

What more could a girl want? Who needs Prince Charming when you can sink into a tub full of piles and piles of fluffy, cloudlike, candy-scented bubbles? Even tough cookies turn into giggling princesses when faced with this pink confection. Luckily the spell wears off and you're left with magically soft, clean skin. Adjust the recipe so everyone can take a bottle home.

Decant the shampoo into the bottles until half-full, add the food coloring, mica, essential oil, and absolute, and cap and shake well. Top up the bottles with shampoo and shake again. Add labels and stickers to the bottles, if you wish. Squirt a generous amount of the bubble bath under running water for bountiful bubbles.

4-ounce jar

¼ cup almond oil

1 tablespoon each dried horsetail, mullein, comfrey, and calendula

¼ cup cocoa butter

1 tablespoon beeswax

A few drops each lemon and tangerine essential oil

Ten ½-ounce balm containers

# lemon drop cuticle balm

Rub a small amount of this lemon-scented soft balm into your cuticles and nails nightly for longer, stronger, more beguiling nails. Horsetail is high in silica and is especially good for nails, mullein is moisturizing, and comfrey and calendula are known for their strong healing abilities.

In the jar, pour the almond oil over the dried herbs, cover, and let infuse for 3 or 4 days, or make a warm oil infusion (page 18) instead. Pour the mixture through a sieve into a liquid measuring cup, removing the plant material and retaining the infused oil. Set aside. Place the cocoa butter and beeswax in a microwave-safe bowl, and microwave on high until melted, about 1 minute. Do not overheat. Using a spoon, stir together the melted mixture, the infused oil, and the essential oils until well blended. Pour the mixture into the containers and let cool completely before capping.

### beauty on the inside:
# ginger cosmopolitans

Spice up that dainty, single-girl elixir for some reckless adventure. A few days before your party, slice and crush a whole, medium-sized gingerroot, place it in a jar, and pour as much vodka over it as you think you'll need for the party. Cap the jar and let it infuse for 3 or 4 days. Pour the vodka through a sieve into a container, removing the ginger and retaining the liquid. If a stronger ginger flavor is desired, repeat the process with fresh ginger added to the same infused vodka.

Mix up an iced shaker of cosmos with 4 parts ginger vodka, 2 parts Cointreau, 1 part fresh lime juice, and 2 parts cranberry juice. Pour into chilled glasses and garnish with a twist of lime.

# glamour on the go

No time for beauty today? Gasp! Where did those fifties
kittens find the time for their extravagant toilette, all
powder puffs, pink poodles, and racy red lips? If you don't
have the patience, the penchant for primping, or the
hours in the day, here are some wash-and-go potions that
will make you look like a bombshell in no time.

These recipes doll-up store-bought products with
invigorating scents and uplifting oils. They are quick to
make and will keep you on your toes. With only a few
minutes of mixing, you'll enjoy la dolce vita with none
of the time-consuming effort. Viva Las Vixens!

# go-go beauty altar

With all the power of the home version but none of the awkward bigness, an on-the-go altar is a more powerful enhancer than a makeup bag.

Find a small matchbox and, using glue, glitz it up on the outside with a color copy of a bad-girl babe, plenty of glitter, and plastic jewels. Repeat the process inside. Then fill your bedazzled box with jinxy items used in beauty spells: a chip of amber, a pinch each of ground cinnamon and flax, a star anise pod, a chip of mirror, a jade bead, a birthday candle, a match, and a few drops of Beauty Temple Incense Oil (page 34). When you're away from home, you can whip out your altar, light the candle, and charm away any glamour emergency.

## beauty on the inside:
## let's go

Whether you love it or avoid it, exercise must happen. If you're always on the go, putting your feet up may sound better than more running around, but exercise is actually relaxing, especially for your mind. Time to zone out and focus on your body and breathing deeply. Still no time? Shake up your routine by changing what you already do into exercise. Run the dog rather than walk, ride your bike to a friend's house, or walk to the store. Fight the boredom of the gym by challenging yourself to work up a sweat with these mysterious activities: capoiera, sivananda, jeet kune do, or paso doble.

8-ounce bottle unscented baby bath soap

8-ounce bottle

A few drops each grapefruit, lime, and tangerine essential oils

Label and stickers (optional)

# speedy shower gel

Invigorating grapefruit will open your eyes and get you out the door in the most pleasant way imaginable. And it takes just seconds to make.

Decant the bath soap into the bottle until half-full. Add the essential oils, cap the bottle, and shake well to combine. Top up the bottle with more soap, cap, and shake again. Add a label and stickers, if you wish.

Note: Dr. Bronner's Baby Soap works really well in this recipe, and it provides you with plenty of reading material, but never mind— you don't have time for that.

¼ cup non-petroleum jelly

A few drops coffee flavoring oil

A few drops flavoring oil to re-create your favorite coffee blend: vanilla, cinnamon, chocolate, hazelnut, or almond (optional)

Eight ¼-ounce lip balm pots

# one-minute-magic
## coffee gloss

Soon you'll need a swipe of this coffee lip gloss each morning just as much as you need your first cup. It takes less time to concoct this gloss and pamper your pucker than to guzzle a cup!

In a small bowl, stir together the non-petroleum jelly and flavoring oils. Spoon the mixture into the lip balm pots.

3/4 cup chamomile tea

2 teaspoons liquid chlorophyll

1 teaspoon liquid vitamin C

1 tablespoon witch hazel

A few drops peppermint or lemon essential oil

8-ounce spritz bottle

# city skin facial spritz

When city grime and stifling smog have got you down, blast them with a fresh spray of vitamins and soothing herbs. This on-call spritz refreshes your tired skin while delivering a powerful boost of antioxidants right where they're needed.

Pour the chamomile tea, chlorophyll, liquid vitamin C, witch hazel, and essential oil into the spritz bottle. Cap tightly and shake well. Stored in the refrigerator, the mixture should remain fresh for 1 month.

# quick cauldron potions

Spend a few quick minutes sniffing to discover your favorite scents. Experiment with blending by dropping a few drops of 2 or 3 essential oils onto a saucer and swirling to blend. Tone down flowery scents with spicy or citrus varieties.

Once you've chosen a few custom perfumes, buy a large bottle of unscented natural lotion, shampoo, massage oil, or conditioner. Baby formulations are often the gentlest and simplest products, and many health food stores have bulk dispensers. Decant the product into a gorgeous new bottle until half-full, add a few drops of the essential oil combo, cap, and shake to blend. Top up the bottle, and shake again.

Add your own custom labels and stickers and hand them out to all your friends. Everyone will think you're so clever. And of course you are!

¼ cup beeswax
¼ cup cocoa butter
¼ cup jojoba oil
¼ cup almond oil
A few drops of your favorite essential oil
Three 2½-ounce push-up deodorant containers

# tah-dah solid lotion

No spills, but plenty of thrills. Lotion in a no-mess tube is a true magic trick. This recipe takes a bit longer to make, but it's worth the time you save in the long run. Slip this divine potion into your book bag for moisture on the go.

In a double boiler set over simmering water, stir together the beeswax and cocoa butter until melted. Remove from the heat and stir the jojoba, almond, and essential oils into the melted mixture. Pour the mixture into the containers and let cool completely before capping.

½ cup filtered water
10-ounce spritz bottle
2 tablespoons witch hazel
A few drops each peppermint, tea tree, and eucalyptus essential oils

# on-your-toes foot spritz

Cute shoes! Adorable, strappy, sexy, irresistible. Sensible? Absolutely not! If your feet have been teetering around, all in the name of cute, pamper them a little before sending them off on their precarious way again with this rejuvenating spritz.

Pour the water into the spritz bottle and add the witch hazel and essential oils. Cap and shake until well blended.

# II

# midsummer night treats

The stars are out, the moon is full, and the witching hour draws near. If your evening includes a moonlit romp through the enchanted woods or a firefly-flecked stroll, a few late-night treats are necessary.

The bedazzling ingredients in these brews will keep you bright-eyed and help you avoid any fairy mischief.

# sweet dreams
## beauty candle

A candle will fire up your charms, especially when it's all dolled up with glitter and jewels. Find a tall votive candle in a glass holder (they are usually decorated with saints). Wrap a color picture of your favorite beauty goddess, from Venus to Venus Williams, around the candle, and tape it in place. Using glue, decorate your deity with tons of glitter and plastic jewels. Place the candle on your Boudoir Altar (page 82) and anoint it with a few drops of Beauty Temple Incense Oil (page 34). Light it during your beauty brewing to add more pow to your potions.

### beauty on the inside:
# star-crossed eye pillows

A scented eye pillow can soothe your eyes and relieve a headache. Fill 2 satin sachets with a few tablespoons of dried lavender. Place one over each eye and lie down.

For a cool treat, fill a snack-sized zip-top plastic bag with a few tablespoons of aloe vera gel. Store it in the refrigerator and place it over your eyes any time they need a recharging rest.

½ teaspoon beeswax
1½ tablespoons coconut oil
1 tablespoon castor oil
2 or 3 drops vitamin E oil
A pinch of cosmetic-grade mica in
a color of your choice
A pinch of cosmetic-grade glitter
1 or 2 drops peppermint essential oil
Two ½-ounce balm containers

# titania's fairy dust
# eye glitter

Glittery, gorgeous, and good for you! A hint of peppermint perks
up your peeps for a night out. Castor oil is especially nourishing
for eyebrows and eyelashes, and no one will guess you're being
so boring and healthy when it's disguised as flashy makeup.

Place the beeswax and coconut oil in a microwave-safe bowl, and
microwave on high until melted, about 1 minute. Do not overheat.
Stir the castor oil, vitamin E oil, mica, glitter, and essential oil into
the melted beeswax until well blended. Pour into the balm
containers and let cool completely before capping.

Note: Peppermint is peppy—in fact, it's just too exuberant for some
skin. Perform a patch test (page 19), and omit the peppermint oil
if irritation occurs. And as with all makeup, do not get this product
in your eyes.

1 cup dark ale
8-ounce bottle
1 lemon

# witching hour hair rinse

Here's a recipe for the late night, pub-hopping heroines who look askance at the girly girls sipping their cosmos. Hearty Irish ale has as much caloric energy as a loaf of bread. You may not need that much oomph for a night out, but your hair might need a swig to swing. Pouring a cosmopolitan over your head won't give you instant sophistication, but the sugars and proteins in a beer rinse will give you shiny, bouncy, voluminous, frizz-free locks. So there!

Pour the beer into a glass, and let it go flat. Real ale does not have added carbonation, so this should only take about 1 hour. Pour the beer into the bottle, add the juice of the lemon, and shake until well blended. After shampooing and conditioning, pour the beer mixture over your head, massaging the rinse through your hair from the scalp to the ends. Wait a few minutes, rinse with tepid water, and towel dry.

1 teaspoon beeswax
1 teaspoon mango butter
1 teaspoon apricot kernel oil
1 teaspoon almond oil
3 or 4 drops vitamin E oil
A few drops of your favorite essential
or flavoring oil (optional)
3 or 4 lip balm tubes

# moonstruck kissing balm

You never know who you'll meet in Oberon's lair. This under-lipstick nourisher plumps up lips for secret kisses. The tube container is easy to keep in a pocket for a late-night swipe of shine.

Place the beeswax and mango butter in a microwave-safe bowl, and microwave on high until melted, about 1 minute. Stir the apricot kernel, almond, vitamin E, and essential oils into the melted mixture. Pour the mixture into the lip balm tubes and let cool completely before capping.

1 cup baking soda

1 cup sodium lauryl sulfoacetate

1 tablespoon cream of tartar

A few tablespoons liquid vegetable glycerin

Food coloring in several colors

A few drops each sandalwood, neroli, and
tangerine essential oils

Latex gloves

# bewitched bubble bar

These solid, colorful bars look as though they're straight from
a funky fairy's Play-Doh Fun Factory, but when mixed with
running water they magically transform into piles of blissful
bubbles. A soothing soak is indispensable before and after a
late night.

In a mixing bowl, stir together the baking soda, lauryl sulfoacetate, and cream of tartar until well blended. Kneading with your hands, slowly add only as much liquid glycerin as necessary to form the powder into a dough. Separate the dough into 3 or 4 pieces, and place each piece into a separate small bowl. Add a few drops of coloring and essential oil to each piece, making each one a different color and scent. Wearing the gloves, knead the color and scent into each. Flatten the balls of dough into equal rectangular shapes, $\frac{1}{4}$ inch thick. Place the rectangles of dough one on top of the other. Roll the dough up like a sushi roll and, using a knife, cut the roll into 1-inch slices. Place the slices on their ends; they should look like colorful spiral-design cookies. Store in a decorative jar, or wrap each one in plastic wrap.

To use, take one slice of bubble bar and hold it under running bath water. It will produce divine-smelling bubbles that grow and grow but don't last very long, so enjoy them while you can, and then soak in the frothy, perfumy tub.

Note: These ingredients are not dangerous, but if you are concerned about dust or are a sneezy type, wear a dust mask and/or work in a well-ventilated space while mixing and measuring the powders.

1 tablespoon rose hip seed oil
2 tablespoons avocado oil
1 tablespoon jojoba oil
2 tablespoons almond oil
Three 1-ounce cobalt blue glass bottles

# stroke-of-midnight makeup remover

Raccoon eyes are sexy in their own rock-star way. But if you're not
out to impress, give your skin a break and remove your makeup
before turning in. Your skin will thank you by behaving itself and
not having a blemish tantrum. The moisturizing oils will nourish
the delicate tissue around the eye without irritating it.

In a small bowl, stir together the rose hip seed, avocado, jojoba, and
almond oils. Decant the mixture into the bottles and cap. Dab a small
amount over your makeup and wipe off with a tissue or soft cloth.

beauty on the inside:
# puck's party cure

It's a fact that staying up into the wee hours is a lot more fun for you than for your body, especially if cocktails are involved. Help your body see things your way by preparing ahead of time. It will thank you in the morning and might even walk you down to the corner for a newspaper without complaint.

Before heading out the door, take a multivitamin with B-complex, and sip cooled herbal tea with a few drops of milk thistle. Then drink a few glasses of water and have an antioxidant-rich glass of juice or a salad.

Once you stumble into the all-night diner, pass on the greasy fries and bad coffee. Opt for cool water with a lemon wedge and oatmeal. Follow up later with a salad of cucumber, pear, and apple, with an acidophilus tablet or some yogurt.

# celtic cures

In the Celtic world, when your milk curdled, your lover quarreled, and blemishes blighted your beauty, the meddlesome fairies were to blame. Today, with barely a buttercup to hide under, the frolicking fairies can take only so much responsibility. But the cures for their curses are still very effective, making the most of folk medicine and herbal lore.

Turn to these quick fixes for immediate problem solvers, from zit zappers to tired eye revivers.

# medieval banishing spell

Show pesky pimples and wanton warts the door. This
medieval banishing spell has a big dash of effective
folk medicine to add to its magical powers. On a night
during the waning moon (this is preferable, although
breakouts wait for no one), slice a garlic clove in half.
Rub the unwelcome wart or blemish with the cut side
of the garlic. Bury the garlic outside while incanting

**as this garlic meets decay**
**so my wart (or blemish) will go away.**

Repeat for 3 nights, or until the problem has healed.

## beauty on the inside:
# tra-la-la

Music soothes the savage beast and the volatile vixen. Toe-
tapping tunes can leave you happy, hectic, or hell-bent. Buy
a new CD for a quick trip to a better mood. Music will renew
your inside while your potions take care of the rest.

Half a small tomato
1 teaspoon lemon juice
1 tablespoon instant oatmeal
2-inch-wide china brush (optional)

# pagan potion mask

Before an important event, you may ask your skin, very nicely,
to behave. "Just one day!" you plead. But your skin always likes
to let you know who's boss. This mask is soothing, healing, and
naturally astringent. It dries out the bad stuff while encouraging
the good stuff. It dishes out just the right kind of punishment
too. What self-respecting, overbearing skin wants to have
tomato rubbed in its face?

Cut the tomato in half and remove the seeds. In a small bowl, mash
the tomato with a fork. Stir the lemon juice and oatmeal into the
tomato mash, blending until the oatmeal plumps up. Using a china
brush or your fingertips, spread an even layer of the mixture over
your face, avoiding the eye area. Relax for 10 minutes. Rinse with
cool water, pat dry, and moisturize if necessary. Toss any leftovers.

8-ounce jar
2 tablespoons tea tree oil
1 teaspoon each dried fennel, yarrow, and chamomile
One 1/3-ounce mini roll-on bottle

# zit zap magic wand

Sometimes skin behaves like a perennial teenager, even when it's 30! Make a magic wand to zap the red out of pimples and stop them in their tracks. Tea tree oil dries up oil and cleanses aggravated areas, while a mix of herbs encourages skin regeneration.

In the jar, pour the tea tree oil over the fennel, yarrow, and chamomile, cover, and let infuse for 3 or 4 days. Pour the mixture through a sieve into a liquid measuring cup, removing the plant material and retaining the infused oil. Pour the infused oil into the roll-on bottle, pop in the roller ball, and cap. Apply a swipe directly to a breakout.

# bright eye soothers

With all that winking and eyelash batting, it's no wonder your eyes need a rest. Revive them to their best flirty form with simple and fresh kitchen cures that address every possible ill.

### puffiness: 2 rose hip tea bags

Place the tea bags in a cup, and pour boiling water over them. When the bags have cooled, wring them out, and place one over each eye. Relax for 15 minutes, and pat dry.

### dark circles: 1 green fig

Slice the fig in half and place one half over each eye. Relax for 15 minutes, rinse, and pat dry.

### irritated: 2 cucumber slices

Place a disk of cucumber over each eye. Relax for 15 minutes, rinse, and pat dry.

### sore and red: 2 potato slices

Place a potato slice over each eye. Relax for 15 minutes, rinse, and pat dry.

### bloodshot: ¼ cup skim milk

Place 2 cotton balls in a saucer of milk, wring them out, and place one over each eye. Relax for 15 minutes, rinse, and pat dry.

# fresh flower **toners**

A little splash after cleansing refreshes the skin, refines pores, and removes any lingering cleanser. Choose one that suits your skin type.

Small jar
3 tablespoons witch hazel
$1/2$ teaspoon cider vinegar
2 tablespoons dried chamomile
1 cup water
1 tablespoon peppermint extract
12-ounce bottle

## normal to oily skin

In the small jar, pour the witch hazel and cider vinegar over the chamomile, cover, and let infuse for 3 or 4 days. Pour the mixture through a sieve into a liquid measuring cup, removing the plant material and retaining the infused liquid. Stir the water and peppermint extract into the infused witch hazel. Decant the mixture into the bottle. The toner should remain fresh for 1 month. Shake before each use, and use a cotton ball to dab it on the face after cleansing.

Small jar

1 cup filtered water

2 tablespoons dried lavender and rose petals

15 drops lavender essential oil

15 drops rose essential oil

8-ounce bottle

## normal to dry skin

In the small jar, pour the water over the lavender and rose petals, add the essential oils, cover, and let infuse for 2 weeks. Pour the mixture through a coffee filter into a liquid measuring cup, removing the plant material and retaining the infused liquid. Decant the infused liquid into the bottle. Use a cotton ball to dab it on the face after cleansing.

Mortar and pestle
1 tablespoon sage leaves
1 tablespoon sea salt
1 or 2 drops peppermint essential oil (optional)
Baking sheet

# twinkle smile polish

Use this powder once a week for the pearly whites of a pinup without the chemicals. This recipe was a favorite of Elizabeth I, but don't expect to see the stunning results in a toothy portrait. The grand dame was no toothpaste model and opted instead for a stern stare. Heck, what do you expect? She had a country to run.

Using a mortar and pestle, crush together the sage leaves and salt until it forms a paste. Add the essential oil, if you wish. Spread the paste on a baking sheet and bake at 250°F until dry, about 15 minutes. Crush the dried paste into a powder and store in an airtight container. Brush your teeth with the powder once a week.

# glamour goddesses

"Love your wrinkles." "You're only as old as you feel." Blah, blah, blah. You've heard this and taken it to heart, but maybe you're not quite ready to let your skin kick back and goof off. It's time to get in on the goddesses' secrets for eternal youth. Those thousand-year-old dames don't let the calendar tell them how to look or feel.

Youthful or wisdomful, you don't have to be at a specific time in life to benefit from these regenerative treatments. Dry skin, tired skin, irritated skin, or just plain normal skin will all enjoy these amazingly soothing serums. Time really is an abstract concept—just ask Venus—so grow up, stop obsessing, and enjoy it.

# juno's three
# rejuvenating masks

Your life has been as smooth and shiny as new Tupperware. When suddenly—hey, what's *that?* That, there on my face! If you've run up against a rough patch or, gasp, a wrinkle, let it know it's not welcome in this house with one of these regenerative masks.

Juno, as the mother of all goddesses, expects to be the shiniest star in the sky. She maintains her radiance with the strongest of ingredients, antioxidant vitamin C, skin-resurfacing citrus, and firming protein.

2 teaspoons plain yogurt
1 teaspoon orange juice
2-inch-wide china brush

## super C mask

A mega-dose of C provides a blast of antioxidants.

In a small bowl, stir together the yogurt and orange juice. Using a china brush or your fingertips, spread an even layer of the mixture over your face, avoiding the eye area. Relax for 5 to 10 minutes, rinse off, pat dry, and moisturize as usual. Toss any leftovers.

Note: The two citrus masks can cause irritation with their heavy dose of citric acid. Perform a patch test (page 19) before trying one on your face. Then begin by leaving the mask on for only a few minutes.

Lemon zester
1 lemon
Cotton balls

# lemon peel mask

Exfoliating skin cells stimulates collagen production and brings
brand-new baby skin to the surface. Coochie-coo.

Zest the lemon's peel into a small bowl, juice the lemon over the
peel, and let infuse in the refrigerator for 30 minutes. Using cotton
balls, dab the lemon juice over your face, avoiding the eye area.
Relax for 5 to 10 minutes, rinse off, pat dry, and moisturize as
usual. Store any leftovers in the refrigerator.

1 tablespoon honey
1 egg white
1 teaspoon liquid vegetable glycerin
1/2 teaspoon cornstarch
2-inch-wide china brush

# firming mask

A quick lift with none of the messy surgery. It might not last as
long, but hey, it doesn't look as weird either.

In a small bowl, stir together the honey, egg white, glycerin, and
cornstarch until smooth and thoroughly blended. Using a china brush
or your fingertips, spread the mixture in an even layer over your face,
avoiding the eye area. Relax for 10 to 15 minutes, rinse off, pat dry,
and moisturize as usual. Toss any leftovers.

# eternal youth spell

A wrinkle here, a line there, may all add up to a crazy
map, and the destination is nowhere you want to go. It's
time to grab the steering wheel and get things back on
the smooth and narrow.

During the waxing moon, sit at your Boudoir Altar (page
82) and light a pink candle. Rub a polished rose quartz or
red jasper stone over any wrinkles or lines you would like
to eliminate. Drop the stone into a bottle of rose water.
Take 7 rose petals and drop them into the rose water
while repeating

> venus, one of beauty fair;
> your loveliness is in the air.
> petals offered up to fate
> revive the spirit and rejuvenate.

Use the enchanted water as a toner after cleansing.

143

3 tablespoons shea or mango butter

3/4 cup jojoba oil

2 tablespoons emulsifying wax (vegetable based)

2 tablespoons stearic acid (derived from vegetable fats)

1 tablespoon rose water, purchased or homemade (see Infused Waters, page 18)

2 cups filtered water

Immersion hand mixer (whisk, hand beater, or blender)

1 tablespoon vitamin E oil (a natural preservative)

1 teaspoon evening primrose essential oil

A few drops of your favorite fragrance or essential oil

Four 8-ounce containers

# venus's magic cream

Every cream must promise something: a new look (much prettier than the one you have), a better life (than what you're calling a life now), and a boyfriend with an accent. This rich cream happens to like you just the way you are (although it's still not sure about the boyfriend). It is so gentle and unassuming that it promises only a small miracle. However, tucked away inside its creamy countenance are super-strength moisturizing and rejuvenating oils perfect for dry or damaged skin. Don't be shocked and have a heart attack (you are old, after all) when your skin, although still quite distinctly yours, is astonishingly smoother, silkier, and revitalized.

In a double boiler set over simmering water, stir together the shea butter, jojoba oil, emulsifying wax, and stearic acid until melted. In a mixing bowl, stir together the rose water and filtered water. Pour a slow stream of the water mixture into the oil mixture while stirring. When the mixture is smooth and thoroughly blended, remove from the heat. Using the immersion hand mixer, blend in the vitamin E oil, essential oil, and fragrance oil until the mixture is fluffy and thickened. Decant the lotion into the containers, let cool slightly before capping, and label if you wish. Stored in a cool spot, the lotion should remain fresh for 1 month. Shake before each use, if necessary.

beauty on the inside:
# now is the time

If you're feeling inordinately old, you're probably just stuck in an old rut. It's time to try something completely new. Make a list of things you've always wanted to do, from marvelous to mundane. From braving the dizzying heights of K2 to trying the cupcakes at the new café down the street. Ever contemplated pink hair, thought about swimming in the ocean in winter, really considered reading *Anna Karenina*? You only live once, as they say, so now is the time to get moving. Try to tick some of the small things off the list, one every other week. Then start getting the big things off the ground, one step at a time. Hike the hill behind the house before heading to Machu Picchu. Learn to paddle a canoe this summer on your way to the Amazon.

1 tablespoon each dried eyebright
and elder flowers

¼ cup boiling filtered water

½ cup aloe vera gel

4-ounce container

# aurora's elder flower
eye gel

When you rise before dawn, as Aurora must, it is no wonder that
your peeps are pooped. Time to lose the lines and perish the puffs.
Your best feature demands the best treatment. Liven them up with
a surge of moisture imbued with therapeutic herbs and flowers.

In a small bowl, pour the boiling water over the eyebright and elder
flowers, cover, and let steep for 10 minutes. Pour the mixture
through a sieve into a small bowl, removing the plant material and
retaining the infused liquid. Measure 1 tablespoon of the infused
liquid into a double boiler set over simmering water, and stir in the
aloe vera gel until thickened. Let cool, and then pour through a
sieve into a small bowl, removing any solids and retaining the gel.
Spoon into the container. Stored in the refrigerator, the gel should
remain fresh for 2 to 3 weeks. Stir before using, if necessary. Dab
a small amount around the eye area daily.

1 tablespoon jojoba oil

2 teaspoons rose hip seed oil

One ½-ounce cobalt blue bottle

3 drops everlast essential oil

3 drops German chamomile essential oil

3 drops evening primrose essential oil

5 drops of your favorite essential oil:
lavender, neroli, or rose absolute

Skewer or toothpick

# flora's blue chamomile face serum

Stop fretting over a random wrinkle; your worrying will only give you more lines. This serum makes use of some of the oldest and still most effective wrinkle-fighting oils. Jojoba is similar to your own skin oils and will not clog pores. Rose hip seed and evening primrose are skin regenerative. Flora's favorite flower, German chamomile, is anti-inflammatory. Deliver a drop of serum straight to the offending line each night before bed or under your makeup each morning.

Pour the jojoba and rose hip seed oil into the bottle, add the essential oils, and stir with a skewer or toothpick.

# queen of sheba spa

Makeda, the Queen of Sheba, was known for her beauty, intelligence, and inquisitive nature. Her life was an adventure from the beginning. As a baby, a mysterious stranger saved her from the sacrificial jaws of a serpent god. She loved learning new things, and her legend is full of fanciful magic carpet rides, pet jackals, talking birds, and trips to distant lands. But despite her hectic life as a monarch, she always knew when to relax, returning home to the shores of the Red Sea to refresh herself.

Appoint yourself Queen of the Spa for the day, and treat yourself to these stress-fighting, pampering elixirs, potions, and brews that will help your body rebalance. Take a day off and try the most calming fragrances in your blends, such as vetiver, chamomile, and ylang-ylang.

# enchanted garden

Start a beauty garden full of herbs and flowers known for their
beautifying properties. Having a window box full of flowers gives you
the chance to nurture their beauty right from the first sprout. Aloe
vera, calendula (marigold), chamomile, clary sage, comfrey, lavender,
lemon balm, peppermint, rosemary, and violet are all hardy, easy-to-
grow aromatics that have multiple uses.

You can extract aloe vera gel by cutting a leaf lengthwise, and
scooping the gel into a small jar. Store it in the refrigerator.

To dry the herbs and flowers, cut the mature stems, tie them
together, and hang them upside down in a dark, well-ventilated area.

# emerald elixir

Spa juice must be emerald green—it's expected! Keep
up appearances by starting your day, at least
occasionally, with this classic ultra-green juice. In a
blender, combine a handful of wheatgrass, a frozen
banana, 1/2 cup apple juice, a tablespoon of spirulina,
and half a mango. It will taste even better if, while
sipping, you close your eyes and imagine your hair in
a towel turban and your feet being massaged. Ah.

4-ounce glass jar

1/2 cup filtered water

10 drops each bergamot and chamomile essential oils and rose absolute

8-ounce spritz bottle

# relaxation facial spritz

The serene scents of this blend are soothing to your body and mind. Bergamot whisks you off on a magic carpet ride, while chamomile makes sure you have a safe landing.

Fill the 4-ounce jar half-full with the water, add the essential oils, cap, and shake. Top up the jar with the remaining water, cap, and shake again. Let infuse for a few weeks, strain through a coffee filter, and decant into the spritz bottle.

beauty on the inside:

## spa day

Plan a day of relaxation—no agenda, just go with your whim. Start off by cleaning up the night before so your mind can be as clear as your tables, floor, and laundry basket. Throw everything in the closet and don't open it for 24 hours. Get up late, sip your bright green elixir, and slip in a CD of that chanting-chime-ringing-raindrop music (or choose something less annoying). Do a few of your most dramatic yoga moves. Then mix up 3 or 4 beauty spells and revamp yourself from top to toe. When you're finished, you will be an irrepressible force of nature, and you'll smell nice too!

8-inch square of cheesecloth

1/2 cup each dried lavender and chamomile

A few drops each ginger, lavender, and sandalwood essential oils and jasmine absolute

6-inch length of lavender ribbon

# tantalizing tea bath

As relaxing as a cup of tea, the calming aroma of this floral bath will inspire the kind of daydreams worth indulging in.

Place the lavender and chamomile in the center of the cheesecloth and add the drops of essential oil to the flowers. Gather up the corners of the cheesecloth and tie with the ribbon. Draw a warm bath and drop the bath bag in. Let it infuse for a few minutes, hop in, and dream.

3 tablespoons oatmeal

1 tablespoon almonds

Spice grinder

1 tablespoon Moroccan red clay (optional)

1½ tablespoons hydrogen peroxide

2 tablespoons filtered water

A few drops of your favorite calming scent, such as vetiver, chamomile, or ylang-ylang essential oil

2-inch-wide china brush (optional)

# red sea facial

Oxygen slows the aging process. Suddenly breathing more deeply? Boost the surface oxygen on your face with this frothy mask. Oatmeal and almonds soothe the skin, while red clay deep-cleanses your pores.

Grind the oatmeal and almonds together in a clean spice grinder. In a small bowl, stir together the oatmeal mixture, clay, hydrogen peroxide, water, and essential oil. Using a china brush or your fingertips, spread an even layer of the mixture over your face, avoiding the eye area. Relax for 5 minutes. Using a circular motion, rub the mask off to exfoliate, rinse with warm water, pat dry, and moisturize as usual. Toss any leftovers.

¼ cup jojoba oil

1 tablespoon emulsifying wax (vegetable based)

1 tablespoon stearic acid (derived from vegetable oil)

1 tablespoon liquid vegetable glycerin

1½ cups filtered water

Immersion hand mixer (hand mixer, blender, or whisk)

¼ teaspoon vitamin E oil (a natural preservative)

A few drops essential oil; try jasmine and lemon or elemi (choose a scent for which you'd like to be notorious)

8-ounce container

# bare-naked body lotion

This may be all you need to wear. A comfy hair-in-a-ponytail, feet-in-bunny-slippers lotion for every day, it's as simple and as good as vanilla ice cream.

In a double boiler set over simmering water, stir together the jojoba oil, emulsifying wax, stearic acid, and glycerin until melted. Pour a slow stream of the water into the oil mixture while stirring. When the mixture is smooth and thoroughly blended, remove from the heat. Using the immersion hand mixer, blend in the vitamin E and essential oils until the mixture is fluffy and thickened. Decant the lotion into the bottle and let cool slightly before capping. Stored in a cool spot, the lotion should remain fresh for 1 month. Shake before each use, if necessary.

notes